Warman's®

Action Figures

FIELD GUIDE

Mark Bellomo

Values and Identification

Published by

krause publications

An Imprint of F+W Publications

700 East State Street • Iola, WI 54990-0001
715-445-2214 • 888-457-2873

Our toll-free number to place an order or obtain a free catalog is
(800) 258-0929.

Library of Congress Catalog Number: 2006922400

ISBN 13: 978-0-89689-420-4
ISBN 10: 0-89689-420-7

Designed by Kay Sanders & Sally Olson
Edited by Karen O'Brien

Printed in China

Contents

Editor's Note: Please read the *How To Use This Book* section before proceeding to your areas of interest as it contains vital information regarding the abbreviations and pricing used throughout this text.

How to Use This Book

This book is a compact introduction to modern action figure toys and a quick reference guide. I included the action figures that are most commonly found on the secondary market.

Therefore, this field guide is an overview of the hobby—an alphabetical listing of action figures produced from 1964 to the present—and is by no means is a complete reference guide. A complete action figure reference guide (1964-2006) would run at least 2,000+ pages and would include a minimum of 3,000+ photos. And you couldn't fit that omnibus encyclopedia in your back pocket, much less in the passenger side of your automobile. Still, this book will identify most domestic action figures made in the last forty years.

I have been collecting toys and action figures for more than twenty years, and hope that my experience will make the book—a labor of true love—a first-rate reference. To wit: each figure pictured in this book is from my personal collection; I have researched each and every toy line personally. Therefore, the toys pictured in this guide are not for sale, but are merely samples and references of those pieces you may encounter in your travels.

Abbreviations

MISB: Mint in Sealed Box. These are very difficult samples to find, especially if the piece is rare already, and from a major toy line. With MISB samples, ALL of the boxed contents are sealed in their appropriate plastic baggies within the box, and the box itself is "factory sealed"—it has never been opened by human hands.

MOMC: Mint on Mint Card.

MIB: Mint in Box. This is an uncommon way to find action figure and action figure vehicle samples. Keep in mind that you must ask if the action figure or toy is MIB and complete—make sure that all the pieces are still included in the box. If you doubt this to be true, go home and research to see if the piece is indeed complete. If not, adjust the value of the sample down according to the rarity of the piece that is missing. "MIP" is another abbreviation that is similar to MIB. MIP stands for "Mint in Package." The same criteria apply here.

You may also want to consider the price of an action figure by observing both the condition of the box and the action figure inside the box separately: if the box is in bad condition, but the figure is in mint condition, you must decide which is more important to you—especially as a buyer: the packaging around the figure or vehicle or accessory, or the figure inside.

On a related note, some collectors actually buy every action figure in their collection in mint, loose, and complete condition and then eventually buy boxes separately in which to package these pieces. Therefore, some of the rarer action figure boxes are actually worth quite a bit of money themselves. I've seen the box for the 3-3/4" G.I. Joe U.S.S. Flagg in excellent and near mint condition sell for $100 alone! And this is without any part of the toy included—but these deals are hard to come by for both buyers and seller, and rarely apply to anyone but the most finicky and die-hard collector.

MOC: Mint on Card. This is an uncommon way to find a carded action figure, but is the condition that many collectors desire to own. If a figure is MOC, make sure there is no lifting of the plastic bubble from the backer card or that the card has not been resealed as it is possible for untrustworthy dealers to reseal a card and call it a true MOC sample. Cards that have been resealed around loose and complete action figures are worth much less than actual, non-removed, and non-resealed MOC figures. If a true MOC 3-3/4" G.I. Joe Cobra Commander figure sells for about $1,000 (depending on the condition of the card), then a resealed Cobra Commander figure will sell for between $100-125—yes, a bit more than what he sells for when the character is mint, loose, and complete, but far less than the true MOC sample.

MLC: Mint, Loose, and Complete. This designation states that an action figure, vehicle, or accessory is in mint condition, is outside of its original packaging, and is complete with all of its parts. Frequently, I will find action figures listed as "MLC" that are not—whether these figures are missing an important part (such as a cape, rifle, etc.), or the figure has a lot of paint wear, loose joints, chipping, etc. It is important to ask questions before buying an expensive figure to make sure it is complete and in good condition, because sometimes (as in the case of some higher-end Transformers) an action figure's accessories are worth as much as the figure itself! If a figure is mint and loose, but not complete, then grade down the price of the toy appropriately. A worn toy with no accessories is rarely worth much money, but this all depends on the rarity of the figure itself. For instance, a vintage 3-3/4" Star Wars Jawa figure missing its cape and gun (all of its accessories) might be a hard sell even at a single dollar, where a stripped-down original Captain Action figure in okay condition is still worth, perhaps $20.

NM: Near Mint. Items in this condition are loose, complete, and not in their original packaging. Not much playwear and almost mint.

Pricing Explanation

The numbers listed in the two columns to the right of each item are values for the item in U.S. dollars. The left column displays the value for **MLC** (Mint, Loose, Complete) condition, while the column on the right displays the item's value in **MIB** or **MIP** (Mint in Box or Mint in Package) condition.

An additional value has been added in parenthesis next to the **MIB** value when there is an additional premium for items that are in **MISB** (Mint in Sealed Box) condition. For example, the listing for the popular Series 1 Transformer character Jazz (found on p. 459) contains values for **MLC** in the left column, and **MIB** followed by **MISB** values in the right column.

The G.I. Joe 12" chapter contains three distinct pricing columns. Values in the left column are for loose items in **NM** (Near Mint) condition. Values in the middle column are for items in **MLC** (Mint, Loose, Complete) condition. Values in the right column are for items in **MIB** or **MIP** (Mint in Box or Mint in Package) condition.

Introduction

Extraordinary People

When I was asked to write the very first *Warman's Action Figure Field Guide*, I immediately became concerned with my introduction to the handy book—and how to draft a brief treatise on my dedication to this amazing hobby. I reflected upon my many articles I have painstakingly crafted over the past few years for *ToyFare* magazine, *Lee's [Action Figure News and] Toy Review*, *Tomart's Action Figure Digest*, and most recently, my wonderful tenure at my absolute favorite collectible publication: *Toy Shop* magazine.

While reminiscing upon my assigned topic, I was reminded of the speech given by *Boston Globe* sports columnist, Peter Gammons, delivered at the Baseball Hall of Fame Induction Ceremony in July of 2005. His opening words stated, "I am here today [to speak to you] because I found what I love... and I am *fortunate enough* to be surrounded by extraordinary people." These extraordinary people have fueled my love for action figure collectibles.

It was my Aunt Marie who, in 1975 bought me my first action figure, a Comic Action Superheroes Hulk, for a whopping 52 cents at a local K-Mart.

It was my Aunt Betty who, on every birthday from 1975-82, let me choose one Mego World's Greatest Superhero from off the racks when making our annual trip to the toy section of a Grant's Department Store.

It was my mother, who despite the loud protests of other parents that thought I was "too old to play with toys," bought me a U.S.S. Flagg playset as my Christmas present in 1985—I was fourteen.

It was my eight-year old friend Andy Lopez who, in 1980, taught me how to scour Little League field bleachers after baseball games to find loose change and fallen dollar bills to finance my obscenely large Smurfs collection—all colors and sizes of their mushroom houses, Gargamel and Azrael, and even a Smurfette playing baseball!

It was my Uncle Johnny who bought me my very first Star Wars 12-back figures (Chewbacca, R2-D2, C-3PO, and Luke Skywalker—mint on German cards) in the muggy summer of 1978. It would be *months* before I was bored enough with these four figures to even think of buying a Darth Vader!

It was my father who encouraged me to spend my birthday money in 1984 on five full sealed cases of Star Wars Power of the Force Collector's Coin figures when they were discounted at Kay-Bee Toy Stores for $1.99 a piece. These figures would become the funds I needed to begin my collecting hobby in earnest—as over the course of the next ten years I sold off my doubles and triples (I never trade or sell anything that I only own one copy of—whether comic book or collectible) for trade to finance other comics and toys. This has now become the way I collect: via a trade and barter system.

I relate these anecdotes to you with the faith that you have your own stories—your own tales that evince your love of collecting, and that you all appreciate the qualities and characteristics that it takes to be an action figure collector.

But what is a collector? And most importantly, why do we collect?

Why Collect?

Even though the occupation, the designation, or the pastime of "collector" came into existence in the year 1865—coined by the French "stamp-collector" Georges Herpin—it is in the last twenty years that America has truly witnessed the "Age of the Collector." With the publication of magazines such as *Toy Shop* (especially in the late 1980s), the boom of collectible and specialty stores in the late 1990s, and the rise of the Internet and its online auction sites in the new millennium, collecting is "in vogue" and highly profitable—to the extent that many cunning and affluent investors forego trading in stocks and bonds in lieu of CGC (Comics Grading Authority) slabbed Golden and Silver Age comic books, and high-grade Action Figure Authority standardized toys and action figures.

And why not? Why shouldn't people invest in rare and high-grade comics and action figures? These are sound investments: the return is likely to be more than what would be garnered from a savings account, or even high-yield (high-risk) stocks, *and* they're tangible—you can hold them in your hands, smell the pages, bend the figure into action poses. Place these objects gently into your safety deposit box, and sit back and count your money once a year. The value of these high-grade items rarely decrease.

Consider the following two cases.

In 1992, *Detective Comics* #27, the first appearance of Batman, was worth $80,000 in Near Mint condition according to *Overstreet's Price Guide*. In 2005, the value of *Detective Comics* #27 in Near Mint was an astounding $375,000. Although less than 100 copies of this comic book exist in the entire world, that's a total profit for the owner of nearly $300,000 in ten years. So of course, many investors are putting their faith into these four-color "funny books" for a handsome return. And you may be able to find a copy of *Detective* #27 available at a major auction house like Sotheby's—perhaps once a year.

For a more personal example, in 2001 I bought a MOC Cobra Commander figure from the first series of the 3-3/4" G.I. Joe line for $50. The card's peg hole (the little tab that is "punched" in order to hang the figure on a toy store wall) was unpunched and the card was in mint condition. I recently saw a professionally graded 1982 Cobra Commander—exactly like my own—sell on eBay in early 2005 for close to $1,600. The moral here is that "regular" people are investing in what once was purely a collector's domain—for good or bad.

But is that what fuels the "die-hard" collector? Profit? Is that why we collect? To make a buck? I've witnessed collectors of every toy line from every different social background imaginable, and the true collectors—the ones who belong to a happier circle and whom I welcome as my sisters and brothers—are *not* motivated by money and greed.

They're motivated by a *particular passion*, a certain unwavering loyalty to a specific brand, or toy line, or comic book character, or cartoon star, or movie hero, etc. Whether you collect comics or die-cast cars or action figures... there is a large amount of passion, devotion, and dedication involved. And not dedication to money, but to a specific arena, be it G.I. Joe, Super Heroes, Strawberry Shortcake, *ad infinitum*.

Exciting Times

We are living during a very exciting time for collectors. More action figure lines from the 1960s through the '90s have experienced a resurgence in the past five years than at any other time in history including He-Man and the Masters of the Universe, Captain Action, Transformers, Teenage Mutant Ninja Turtles, Star Wars, etc. We are very lucky hobbyists, indeed.

The world and the secondary marketplace have changed for collectors in modern America. But as the world has changed, it seems collecting has been embraced by more and more people, and collecting is now more than a lifestyle, it is a way of life.

Now our iconic collectibles are touchstones—they are the signifiers, the signified, and the signs that create meaning in a pop-culture saturated America—they connote and denote. And further, collectibles act as a way of creating meaning with others.

Regardless of the action figure, the colorful names of collectible toy lines conjure up memories, emotions, and are iconic touchstones that take collectors into the past.

And that is what I hope I have accomplished with this field guide: I hope I have led you to reflect about your past as a collector, and that I have left you a little bit happier than you were before this purchase.

Thank you all for your kind attention, and I hope to see you upon the release of my next book, *Transformers G1*.

Mark W. Bellomo

Angel
(Moore Action Collectibles, 2002-04; Diamond Collectibles, 2004+)

Series 1

Angel	6	25
Cordelia	8	30
Cordelia (red shirt with short hair; summer show exclusive)	8	30
Faith	8	30
Faith (with leather jacket; Action Figure Express exclusive)	8	30
Slave Cordelia (boxed; Toyfare exclusive)	5	15
Slave Cordelia (carded; Suncoast exclusive)	5	15
Vampire Angel (Diamond exclusive)	10-12	25
Vampire Angel (with leather jacket, M.A.C. Collector's Club exclusive)	6	25

Series 2

Lorne (Vegas; "The House Always Wins" Time and Space Toys Wizard World Chicago exclusive)	6	25
Lorne (red suit; "There's No Place Like Plrtz Glrb" chase figure)	6	25
Lorne (white jacket)	5	15
Wesley ("Bad Girls"; Diamond exclusive)	4	12
Wesley ("Parting Gifts"; Toyfare exclusive)	5	20
Wesley ("Rain of Fire"; Time and Space Toys exclusive)	5	20
Wesley ("Season Four")	4	12
Wesley ("Waiting in the Wings"; Tower Records exclusive)	4	12
Wesley, unpainted (Wizard World Philadelphia exclusive)	10	30

Series 3

Angel ("Season Five")	6	15

Angel, Angel "Season 5," Series 3, Moore Action Collectibles, 2004, $15 MOC.

Angel ("The Ring"; Action Figure Express exclusive)	6	16
Angel ("Graduation Day"; Suncoast exclusive)	6	16
Fred ("Season Three")	6	15
Illyria (Diamond exclusive)	6	15
Illyria ("Shells")	6	20
Pylean Demon Angel (Time and Space Toys exclusive)	6	15
Vampire Angel with baby Connor (Tower Records exclusive)	6	16

Batman
(Mattel, 2003-04)

Arctic Shield Batman	5	10
Battle Armor Batman	5	10
Battle Board Robin	5	10
Battle Board Robin (repaint)	8-10	15-18
Battle Spike Batman	5	10
Croc Armor Batman	5	10
Drill Cannon Batman	5	10
Electro-Net Batman	5	10
Hydro-Suit Batman	5	10
Ice Cannon Mr. Freeze	5-6	12-14
Ice Cannon Mr. Freeze (without goggles)	10-15	20-25
Killer Croc	8	15-18
Martial Arts Batman	5	10
Night Patrol Batman (deluxe)	5	10
Quick Fire Joker	6-8	10-12
Sky Strike Batman (deluxe)	5	10
Sling Strike Nightwing	5-6	10-12
Snare Strike Batman	5	10
Stealth Armor Batman (deluxe)	5	10
Tech Armor Batman (deluxe)	5	10
Zipline Batman	5	10

BTAS, Combat Belt Batman, Series 1, Kenner, 1992, $18-25 MOC.

Multi-packs

Attack of the Penguin (2004, animated Batgirl, Batman, Nightwing, Penguin)	15	30
Batman and Nightwing (2003, animated or new sculpt)	10	15
Batman and Robin (2003, animated)	5	10
Batman and Superman (2003, new sculpt)	10	15
Batman versus Joker (2003, animated)	7	12
Battle Armor Batman and Quick Fire Joker (2004)	10	20
Battle Scars: Batman vs. Catwoman (2003, animated)	7	12
Gotham City Figures (2004, Batman, Catwoman, Joker, Two-Face)	12	25
Tech-Suit Batman versus Two-Face (2003, animated)	7	12
Zipline Batman and Battle Board Robin (2004)	10	20

Vehicles

Batcopter (2003, "fixed" Batman figure)	12	22
Batcycle (2003, "fixed" Batman figure)	10	20
Batjet (2003, with Batman figure)	10	20
Batmobile (2003, recalled)	10	25
Batplane (2003, with Batman figure)	10	20

Batman: Animated Series, The

(Kenner, 1992-2000; Hasbro, 2000-02)

It must be noted that many dealers artificially inflate the prices of BTAS figures and vehicles based on a once-high demand for *some* Batman pieces during the late 1980s and early '90s. Unfortunately, even though there was a small push for the character and his plastic products around the time of the release of *Batman Begins* (2005), the bountiful supply of these figures on pegs and in retail stores belies the fact that there exists no true dearth of these toys. Couple that with the lack of demand from those rare collectors who wish to acquire "every single Batman toy"—and adjust inflated prices accordingly.

BTAS, Batmobile, Series 1, Kenner, 1992, $35-40 MIB.

Again, I cannot stress enough the fact that many secondary and online stores mark these pieces up to double, triple, or even quadruple the value of what they are actually worth. A quick "Completed Items" search on eBay reveals the true prices of these pieces (and remember to add that $3-5 shipping).

BTAS figures were made by Kenner and produced under the Kenner name until Hasbro (who has owned the company since mid-1991) made label changes and switched to their own logo on BTAS packages in 2000. Hasbro lost the license to produce Batman toys in 2002, and then Mattel picked up the license.

Series 1 (1992)

Combat Belt Batman	10	18-25
Penguin	10	35-40
Riddler	6	12-15
Robin	5	8-12
Turbojet Batman	6	8-12
Two-Face	6	15-22

Vehicles

Aerobat	10	22-25
Batcycle	10	20
Batmobile	12	35-40
Bat-Signal Jet	10	20
B.A.T.V. Vehicle	10	20
Crime Stalker	10	20
Hoverbat Vehicle	5	15
Jokermobile	10	20
Robin Dragster	125+	300+
Turbo Batplane	5-6	15

Series 2 (1993)

Bruce Wayne	5	10
Catwoman	5-7	12-15
Infrared Batman	5	10
Joker	5	10
Man-Bat	5-7	12-15

This 2005 Toy Fair Exclusive Batman Begins currently goes for $25 among collectors.

Ninja Robin	5-7	10
Scarecrow	5-7	10-12
Skydive Batman	5	10

Vehicles

Street Jet with Bruce Wayne	12	20-25

Series 3 (1994)

Anti-Freeze Batman	5-7	10
Clayface	5-7	12-15
Dick Grayson	5-7	10
Killer Croc	5-7	10
Knight Star Batman	5-7	10
Lightning Strike Batman	5-7	10 .
Mr. Freeze	4-5	8-10
Ninja Batman and Robin (2-pack)	10	20
Poison Ivy	6-8	15-20

Deluxe figures

Ground Assault Batman	5	10
High Wire Batman	6-8	12-15
Mech-Wing Batman	4-5	10
Power Vision Batman	6-8	12-15

Vehicles

Ice Hammer	10	15

Series 4 (1994)

Bane (Note: large card)	5	10-12
Batman (mail-away, with Battle Helmet)	8-10	25
Cyber Gear Batman	10	15
Radar Scope Batman	10	15
Rapid Attack Batman	10	20
Robin (with Turbo Glider)	5	10-12
Tornado Batman	5	10
Total Armor Batman	5	10

Batman: Mask of the Phantasm, Phantasm, Kenner, 1994, $25 MOC.

Batman: Mask of the Phantasm (1994)

Decoy Batman	10	20
Jet Pack Joker (green face)	10	20
Jet Pack Joker (white face)	10	20
Phantasm	10-12	20-25
Rapid Attack Batman	10	20
Retro Batman	12	25
Tornado Batman	10	20
Total Armor Batman	5	10

Batman: Crime Squad (1995-1996)

Series 1 (1995)

Air Assault Batman	5	10-12
Land Strike Batman	5	10-12
Piranha Blade Batman	5	10-12
Sea Claw Batman	5	10-12
Ski-Blast Robin	5	10-12
Stealthwing Batman	5	10-12
Torpedo Batman	5	10-12

Vehicles

Batcycle	8-10	18-20
Triple Attack Jet	5-7	15

Series 2 (1996)

Bomb Control Batman	10	22-25
Disaster Control Batman	10	22-25
Fast Pursuit Batman	8-10	12-15
Supersonic Batman	8-10	12-15

Deluxe figures

Skycopter Batman	10-12	22-25
Tri-Wing Batman	10-12	22-25

BTAS Multi Packs, Revenge of the Penguin and Shadows of Gotham City, Hasbro, 2002-03, $20ea MIB.

Batman: The Animated Series Multi-Packs

(Toys 'R Us Exclusives; Hasbro, 2002-03)

Alliance of Fear (Batgirl, Batman, Joker, Scarecrow)	3-4 ea.	20
Garden of Evil (Batman, Poison Ivy, Robin)	3-4 ea.	20
Gotham City Enforcement Team (Batgirl, Batman, Commissioner Gordon, Nightwing)	3-4 ea.	20
Puppets of Crime (Batman, Killer Croc, Nightwing, Ventriloquist)	3-4 ea.	20
Revenge of the Penguin (Batman, Catwoman, Robin, The Penguin)	3-4 ea.	20
Shadows of Gotham City (Batman, Ra's Al Ghul, Robin, Talia)	3-4 ea.	20

Vehicles and Playsets

Darkstorm Batcave	25-30	50
Darkstorm Batplane	10-12	20
Darkstorm Batmobile	10-12	20
Shadowcast Batcave	25-30	50
Shadowcast Batmobile	10-12	20
Shadowcast Batplane	10-12	20

Batman: Adventures of Batman and Robin, The (1996-97)

Series 1 (1996)

Bane	8-10	15-20
Hover Jet Batman	5	10
Paraglide Batman	8	15-18
Pogo Stick Joker	5	10
Ra's Al Ghul	8	12-15
Rocketpack Batman	8	20

Vehicles

Nightsphere	15-20	40-45

Batman: The Adventures of Batman and Robin, Harley Quinn (first), Kenner, 1997, $12-15 MOC.

Series 2 (1997)

Bola Trap Robin	5	10
Harley Quinn	5-6	12-15
Joker, "Machine Gun"	8-10	15-20

Duo-Force
(counted as part of "The Adventures of Batman and Robin" series)

Series 1

Air Strike Robin	6-8	10-12
Mr. Freeze	6-8	10-12
Turbo Surge Batman	6-8	10-12
Vector Wing Batman	6-8	10-12

Series 2

Cycle Thruster Batman	6-8	10-12
Hydro Storm Robin	6-8	10-12
The Riddler Roto-Chopper	8-10	12-15
Wind Blitz Batgirl	6-8	12-15

Multi-packs

Rogues Gallery (the first BTAS multi-pack, and it sold *quite* well. Released because of the high demand for short-packed villains since the inception of the line in 1992). The 8-pack includes: Catwoman, Killer Croc, Man-Bat, Poison Ivy, Scarecrow, Joker, Phantasm, Clayface	5 ea.	40-45

Batman: The New Batman Adventures (1997-2000)

Series 1 (1997)

Crime Fighter Robin	5	12
Crime Solver Nightwing	5	12
Detective Batman	6-8	12-15
Mad Hatter	5-6	12-15

Batman: The New Batman Adventures, Bruce Wayne, Series 2, Kenner, 1998, $12 MOC.

Series 2 (1998)

Bruce Wayne	5	12
Force Shield Nightwing	4	10
Knight Glider Batman	5	12
The Creeper	5	12
Wild Card Joker	5-8	12-15
Street Strike Batman	4	10

Multi-packs

Arkham Asylum Escape (four-pack; includes: Batman, Harley Quinn, Poison Ivy, Two Face)	5 ea.	35-40
Arkham Asylum Escape: Batman versus Two-Face (2000)	5 ea.	12-15
Batman and Robin (2000, Wal-Mart exclusive)	5 ea.	12-15
Batman and Superman (2000, Wal-Mart exclusive)	5 ea.	12-15
Batman (New Batman Adventures four-pack; includes: Alfred, Batman, Clayface, Robin)	5 ea.	18-22
Batman versus Joker (2000, Wal-Mart exclusive)	5 ea.	12-15
Knight Force (four-pack; includes: Batgirl, Batman, Nightwing, Robin)	5 ea.	18-25
World's Finest: Batman and Superman (2000, Wal-Mart exclusive)	5 ea.	15-18

Vehicles

Batmobile	12-15	25-30
Batmobile Knightstriker	8-10	15-20
Gotham City Bank	8-10	18-20
Joker Toxic Lab	8-10	18-20

Batman: The New Batman Adventures (1998-99; 12" figures)

Batgirl (Internet exclusive)	10-12	20-25
Batman	12-15	25-30
Harley Quinn	10-12	20-25

Batman: Mission Masters, Rumble Ready Riddler, Series 1, Hasbro, 1997, $8-12 MOC.

Joker	12-15	28-32
Nightwing	10-12	20-25
Robin	12-15	28-32

Batman: Mission Masters (1997-2002)

Although not *actually* part of BTAS, I included these figures with BTAS because they share molds and themes with the line. Sadly, these figures are some of the LEAST desirable of all Batman products and all of the following prices should be used as a *guide* only. Frequently, Mission Masters figures sell in lots for $2-4 apiece because of their (frequently) bright colors, odd accessories, strange names (i.e. "Slalom Racer Batman"), and lack of substantial villains or short-packed figures. These toys were obviously made expressly for a younger demographic rather than the average collector.

Series 1

Anti-Blaze Batman	3	8
Arctic Blast Robin	3	8
Cave Climber Batman	3	8
Desert Attack Batman	3	8
Glider Strike Batman	3	8
Hydrojet Nightwing (deluxe)	5-6	12-15
Insect-Body Mr. Freeze	5-6	8-12
Jungle Tracker Batman	3	8
Mr. Freeze	5-6	8-12
Rumble Ready Riddler	5-6	8-12
Silver Defender Batman (deluxe)	5-6	12-15
Slalom Racer Batman	3	8
Speedboat Batman	3	8

Series 2

Arctic Ambush Robin	6	10-12
Desert Attack Batman	4	8
Hydro Assault Joker	4	8
Knight Strike Batman	4	8
Land Strike Batman	4	8

Batman: Mission Masters, Knight Assault Batman, Series 3, Hasbro, 1999, $8 MOC.

Radar Batman (deluxe)	4	8
Sea Claw Batman	5	8-10
Skychopper Batman (deluxe)	4	8

Series 3

Capture Cape Batman	4	8
Firewing Batman	4	8
Freestyle Skate Batman	4	8
Gotham Crusader Batman	4	8
Ground Pursuit Batman	4	8
Highwire Zip Line Batman	4	8
Inferno Extinction Batman	4	8
Knight Assault Batman	4	8
Mountain Pursuit Batman	4	8
Quick Attack Batman	4	8
Sky Attack Batman	4	8
Virus Attack Mr. Freeze	5-6	10
Virus Delete Batman	4	8

Series 4

Attack Wing Batman	4	8
Battle Staff Batman	4	8
Jet Wing Batman	4	8
Lunar Force Batman	4	8
Midnight Hunter Batman	4	8
Midnight Pursuit Batman (deluxe)	4	8
Midnight Rescue Batman	4	8
Night Assault Batman	4	8
Night Fury Robin	4	8
Night Shadow Batman	4	8
Night Spark Joker	5-6	10
Photon Armor Batman	4	8
Rocket Blast Mr. Freeze	5-6	10
Shadow Blast Batman (deluxe)	4	8

Shadow Copter Batman (deluxe)	4	8
Tunnel Racer Batman	4	8
Turbo Force Nightwing (deluxe)	4-5	8-10
Velocity Storm Batman	4	8

Multi-packs

Joker and Batman	2-3 ea.	10-12
Night Fury Robin and Night Shadow Batman	2-3 ea.	10-12

Vehicles

B.A.T.V. (Batman All-Terrain Vehicle and projectile launcher)	10	20
Hoverbat	10	20
Team Batcycle	12-15	20-25

Batman Beyond
(Hasbro, 1999-2001)

Based on the *Batman Beyond* animated series by Warner Brothers, this cartoon was a younger, hipper, futuristic departure from the more classic *Batman: The Animated Series* and *Batman: The New Adventures*—and the toys initially sold very well. However, on the secondary market, most Batman Beyond product is not worth much money and is usually sold in lots at discount prices.

Ballistic Blade Batman	10	15
Bat Hang Batman	10	15
Blight	12-14	20
Covert Batman	5-7	12
Energy Strike Batman	5-7	12
Future Knight Batman	10	15
Hydro-Force Batman	5-7	12
J's Gang Power Throw	5-7	12
Laser Batman	5-7	12
Lightning Storm Batman	5-7	12
Manta Racer Batman	5-7	12
Neon Camo Batman	3-5	8
Power Armor Batman	8-10	12-15

Power Cape Batman	8-10	12-15
Sonar Strike Batman	5-7	12
Strato Defense Batman	3-5	8
Strikecycle Batman	3-5	8
Surface-to-Air Batman	3-5	8
The Jokerz (with Assault Hover Cycle)	12-15	20-22
Tomorrow Armor Batman	5-7	12

Vehicles

Street-to-Sky Batmobile	10	20

Batman Beyond: Batlink
(Hasbro, 2000-01)

Circuitry Storm Batman	5	10
Codebuster Batman	5	10
Energy Surge Batman	5	10
Firewall Robin	5	10
Mainframe Attack Batman	5	10
Particle Burst Batman	7	12
Power Grid Batman	5	10
Search Engine Batman	7	12
Virtual Joker	5	10

Vehicles

Net Escape Playset	10	20
Netrunner Batmobile	10	15
Virtual Bat	5-7	12

Batman Beyond: Return of the Joker
(Hasbro, 2000)

Arkham Assault Joker	10	15
Golden Armor Batman	10	15
Gotham Defender Batman	5-7	12
Gotham Knight Batman	10-12	18-20
Rapid Switch Bruce Wayne	5-7	12

Batman: Dark Knight Collection, The
(Kenner, 1990-91)

Series 1 (1990)

Bruce Wayne	10	20
Crime Attack Batman	10	20
Iron Winch Batman	10	20
Shadow-Wing Batman	10	20
Sky Escape Joker	15	25
Tec-Shield Batman (black pull)	15	25
Tec-Shield Batman (gold pull)	10	20
Wall Scaler Batman	10	20

Vehicles

Batcopter	35-40	60
Batcycle	20	40
Batjet	35-40	60
Batmobile	40	75
Batwing	20	40
Joker Cycle	10	20

Series 2 (1991)

Knock-Out Joker	15	45
Power Wing Batman	12	25
Thunder Whip Batman	12	25

Deluxe figures

Blast-Shield Batman	12	25
Claw-Climber Batman	12	25
Night-Glider Batman	20	35

Vehicles and Playsets

Bola Bullet	10-15	25
Sky Blade	35-40	60
Strike-Wing	15-20	35

Batman, Knight Force Ninjas (1998)

Series 1

Batman versus the Joker, hand-to-hand combat set	8	15-18
Karate Chop Batman	3	10
Power Kick Batman	3	10
Slide Strike Robin	3	10
Tail Whip Killer Croc	3	10

Series 2

Batman Ally Azreal	3	15
Fist Fury Batman	3	20
Thunder Kick Batman	3	10
Tornado Blade Riddler	3	10

Series 3

Arsenal Cape Batman	7	12
Hyper Crush Robin	7	10
Knight Blade Batman	7	12

Deluxe figures

Multi-Blast Batman	7	12-15

Vehicles

Batmobile (Wal-Mart exclusive, with figure)	12-15	25-30
Knight Force Batmobile	5	15

Batman: Legends of Batman

(Kenner, 1994-96)

Note: It is fairly difficult to find carded specimens from this Batman line in mint condition, so be careful to downgrade prices for "less than excellent condition" packaging.

Series 1 (1994)

Catwoman	7	12
Crusader Batman	10	20
Cyborg Batman	10	15

Dark Riddler Batman	15	30
Future Batman	10	15
Knightquest Batman	10	20
Nightwing	7	12
Power Guardian Batman	10	15
The Joker	10	15
The Riddler	7	12

Series 2 (1995)

Crusader Robin	7	12
Dark Warrior Batman	10	15
Desert Knight Batman (deluxe)	15-18	32-35
Flightpack Batman (deluxe)	18-20	32-35
Knightsend Batman	10	20
Longbow Batman	7	12
Samurai Batman	7	12
Silver Knight Batman (deluxe)	15-18	32-35
Viking Batman	7	12

Series 3 (1996)

Buccaneer Batman	7	12
Energy Surge Batman (deluxe)	10	15-22
First Mate Robin	7	12
Gladiator Batman	7	12
The Laughing Man Joker	7	12
Ultra Armor Batman	10	15-22

Multi-packs

Egyptian Batman and Egyptian Catwoman	10	20
Pirate Batman and Pirate Two-Face	10	20

Vehicles

Batcycle	10	25
Batmobile	10	25
Batmobile with flames	25-30	55-60
Sky Bat	15-18	30-35

Batman, Legends of the Dark Knight
(Kenner, 1996-98)

Series 1
Assault Gauntlet Batman	3	10
Dive Claw Robin (brown or black hair)	5	15
Lethal Impact Bane	3	10
Neural Claw Batman	5	10
Spine Cape Batman	5	10
Twister Strike Scarecrow	3	10

Vehicles
Skywing Street Bike	15-18	25-28

Series 2
Bat Attack Batman	3	10
Glacier Shield Batman	3	10
Laughing Gas Joker	5	10
Panther Prowl Catwoman	5	15

Series 3
Jungle Rage Robin	3	10
Man-Bat	5	15
Penguin	3	10
Underwater Assault Batman	3	10

Series 4
Batgirl	5	15
Dark Knight Batman (blue and gray costume)	15-18	35-38
Dark Knight Batman (black costume, reissue)	15-18	42-45
Lava Fury Batman	3	10

Internet exclusive figures
Dark Knight Detective Batman	15	25
Clayface	8	25
Shatterblade Batman	5	10

Batman: Legends of the Dark Knight, Clayface, Kenner, 1998, $25 MOC.

Batman Begins
(Mattel, 2005)

All figures and vehicles sell for original retail price upon their release, none have increased on the secondary market as of yet.

Batman and Robin
(Kenner, 1997)

Series 1

Bane	3	8
Batgirl	3	5
Battle Gear Bruce Wayne	3	8
Heat Scan Batman	3	8
Hover Attack Batman	3	8
Iceblast Mr. Freeze	7	12
Iceboard Robin	3	5
Jungle Venom Poison Ivy	3	5
Razor Skate Robin	3	5

Series 2

Ambush Attack Batman	3	8
Attack Wing Robin (with ring)	3	8
Battle Board Batman (with ring)	3	8
Blade Blast Robin	3	8
Frostbite	3	8
Ice Blade Batman	3	8
Ice Blade Batman (with ring)	3	13
Jet Wing Mr. Freeze (with ring)	10	20
Laser Cape Batman (with ring)	3	8
Neon Armor Batman	3	8
Neon Armor Batman (with ring)	3	13
Rotoblade Batman (with ring)	3	13
Sky Assault Batman (with ring)	3	13
Snow Tracker Batman	3	8

Talon Strike Robin	3	5
Talon Strike Robin (with ring)	3	10
Thermal Shield Batman (with ring)	3	13
Triple Strike Robin	3	13
Triple Strike Robin (with ring)	3	13
Wing Blast Batman	3	8
Wing Blast Batman (with ring)	3	13

Aerial Defenders (figures)

Aerial Combat Batman	10	20
Aerial Combat Robin	10	20

Deluxe figures

Batgirl with Icestrike Cycle	10	20
Blast Wing Batman	5	8
Blast Wing Robin	5	8
Glacier Battle Robin	5	13
Ice Terror Mr. Freeze	5	8
Redbird Cycle Robin	10	20
Rooftop Pursuit Batman	5	8

Mail-aways

Batman (Fuji Film)	18-20	35

Two-pack figures

A Cold Night at Gotham	5	10
Batman versus Poison Ivy	20	40
Brain versus Brawn	5	10
Challengers of the Night	10	15
Guardians of Gotham	5	10
Night Hunter Robin versus Evil Entrapment Poison Ivy	5	8

12" figures

Batgirl	15	35
Batman	13	25
Batman and Poison Ivy	20	40

Ice Battle Batman (Warner Brothers exclusive)	10	25
Mr. Freeze	10	20
Robin	13	23
Ultimate Batman	8	20
Ultimate Robin	8	20

Vehicles and Playsets

Batmobile	8	20
Cryo Freeze Chamber	3	8
Ice Fortress	5	8
Iceglow Bathammer	25	50
Ice Hammer	10	20
Jet Blade	8	20
Nightsphere	10	25
Sonic Batmobile	8	15
Wayne Manor Batcave	23	53

Batman Forever
(Kenner, 1995)

Series 1

Blast Cape Batman	10	15
Bruce Wayne/Batman (Target exclusive)	15-18	35
Fireguard Batman	10	15
Hydro Claw Robin	10	15
Manta Ray Batman	10	15
Night Flight Batman	10	20
Night Hunter Batman	10	15
Sonar Sensor Batman	10	15
Street Biker Robin	10	15
The Riddler with Question Mark Bazooka	4	12
Tide Racer Robin (Target exclusive)	10	20
Transforming Bruce Wayne (Target exclusive)	10	15
Transforming Dick Grayson	10	15
Two Face	10	15

Series 2

Attack Wing Batman (deluxe)	10	25
Batarang Batman	7	12
Iceblade Batman	7	12
Laser Disk Batman (deluxe)	10	25
Lightwing Batman (deluxe)	10	25
Martial Arts Robin (deluxe)	10	15
Neon Armor Batman	10	15
Night Flight Batman	10	20
Power Beacon Batman	10	15
Recon Hunter Batman	10	15
Riddler with Brain Drain helmet, green figure (silver trim)	15-18	35
Riddler with Brain Drain helmet, green figure (black trim)	3	10
Skyboard Robin	10	15
Solar Shield Batman	10	15
Street Racer Batman	10	15
The Talking Riddler (deluxe)	10	20
Triple Strike Robin	7	12
Wing Blast Batman	10	15

Multi-packs

Batman versus the Riddler	15-20	35
Guardians of Gotham City (Batman and Robin)	15-20	35
Riddler and Two-Face	15-20	35

Vehicles

Batboat	15	25
Batcave	25	50
Batman Power Center	5	10
Batmobile	20	40
Batwing	10	25
Riddler Power Center	5	10

Robin Cycle	7	12
Triple Action Vehicle Set	20	40
Wayne Manor	25	50

Batman Returns
(Kenner, 1992)

Aerostrike Batman	5	15
Air Attack Batman	4	15
Arctic Batman	4	15
Batman, 16"	25	65
Bruce Wayne	10	20
Catwoman	5	15
Crime Attack Batman	4	15
Deep Dive Batman	5	15
Fire Bolt Batman (deluxe)	20	40
Hydrocharge Batman	4	15
Jungle Tracker Batman	4	15
Laser Batman	4	15
Night Climber Batman	4	15
Penguin	12	35
Penguin Commandos	6-8	20
Polar Blast Batman (Toys 'R Us)	4	15
Powerwing Batman	6	15
Robin	10	22
Rocket Blast Batman (Toys 'R Us; deluxe)	15-18	35
Shadow Wing Batman	4	15
Sky Winch Batman	4	15
Thunder Strike Batman	4	15
Thunder Whip Batman	5	15

Vehicles

All-Terrian Batskiboat	25	50
Batcave Command	40	80
Batmobile	35-40	100

The Batman, EXP Clayface, Mattel, 2005, $10 MOC.

Batmobile ("Batmissile")	50	125
Bruce Wayne Custom Coupe	12	40
Camo Attack Batmobile	30	100
Laser Blade Cycle	10-15	25
Penguin Umbrella Jet	15	30
Robin Jetfoil	10	25
Skyblade	25	50
Sky Drop Airship	15	30
Turbo Jet Batwing	30	70

Batman, Movie Collection
(Kenner, 1997)

Batman versus Catwoman	10	22-25
Batman versus Joker	10	22-25
Batman versus Riddler	10	22-25

Batman: Spectrum of the Bat
(Hasbro, 2000-01)

All figures and vehicles sell for original retail price upon their release, none have increased on the secondary market as of yet, as these are re-makes and re-colors of BTAS.

Batman: 100th Edition Figure
(Hasbro, 2001)

Because it comes with (and depends upon) its base, the only specimens will be packaged MIP.   n/a   15

Batman: 200th Edition Figure
(Hasbro, 2001)

	10	20

Batman: World of Batman
(Hasbro, 2001)

All figures and vehicles sell for original retail price upon their release, none have increased on the secondary market as of yet, as these are re-makes and re-colors of BTAS.

Battle Beasts

(Hasbro, 1987)

Figures, individually priced loose—make sure that the rubsigns for these figures are intact before purchasing them—deduct $1-2 per piece if the rubsign is not present or if it is damaged. Carded two-pack prices vary and increase exponentially—sometimes up to $50 (averaging $30-35) each depending on the rarity of the figures packaged inside, especially Series 3 two-packed figures ($60-70). Further, the Laser Beasts are *impossibly* rare, and carded figures are near-impossible to find in any condition.

Series 1

Note: The prices below are for loose figures with weapons. Figures without weapons sell for considerably less.

1 Pirate Lion	5-8
2 Deer Stalker	7-9
3 Ferocious Tiger	6-8
4 Colonel Bird	5-6
5 Killer Carp	6-8
6 Triple Threat Snake	5-7
7 Horny Toad	5-6
8 Sledgehammer Elephant	5-6
9 Rocky Rhino	5-6
10 Roamin Buffalo	7-9
11 Grizzly Bear	5-6
12 Blitzkrieg Bat	6-8
13 Gargantuan Gorilla	11-13
14 Swiny Boar	7-9
15 Gruesome Gator	10-12
16 Sly Fox	7-9
17 Hardtop Tortoise	7-9
18 Rubberneck Giraffe	7-9
19 Prickly Porcupine	10-12
20 Sawtooth Shark	10-12
21 Danger Dog	10-12

22 Hare Razing Rabbit	8-10
23 Sir Sire Horse	7-9
24 War Weasel	10-12
25 Bloodthirsty Bison	7-9
26 Bighorn Sheep	10-12
27 Websligner Spider	8-10
28 Crusty Crab	10-12

Series 2

29 Icky Iguana	10-12
30 Armored Armadillo	8-10
31 Jaded Jaguar (red armor)	7-9
Jaded Jaguar (blue armor)	20-25
32 Humongous Hippo	7-9
33 Major Moose	6-8
34 Delta Chameleon	6-8
35 Kickback Kangaroo	10-12
36 Octillion Octopus	7-9
37 Wolfgang Walrus	7-9
38 Powerhouse Mouse	6-8
39 Dragoon Raccoon	10-12
40 Artic Anteater	6-8
41 Run Amuck Duck	10-12
42 Miner Mole (purple armor)	7-9
Miner Mole (black armor)	15-18
43 Cutthroat Cuttlefish	10-12
44 Eager Beaver	7-9
45 Slasher Sea Horse	10-12
46 Knight Owl	10-12
47 Hunchback Camel	10-12
48 Pillaging Polar Bear	15-20
49 Squire Squirrel	10-12
50 Sabre Sword Tiger	10-12
51 Bludgeoning Bulldog	7-9
52 Pew-trid Skunk	7-9

Series 3

53 Panzer Panda	13-16
54 Leapin' Lizard	7-9
55 Killer Koala	10-12
56 Tarsier Tyrant	10-12
57 Black Panther	12-15
58 Torrential Tapir	10-12
59 King Cobra	15-20
60 Maniac Mandrill	7-9
61 Pixilated Pointer	10-12
62 Pillager Pig	7-9
63 Rowdy Rooster	7-9
64 Musky Ox	7-9
65 Tanglin Pangolin	15-20
66 Slowpoke Sloth	10-12
67 Ardent Aardvark	10-12
68 Bodacious Bovine	15-20
69 Zealot Zebra	15-20
70 Harrier Hawk	15-20
71 Diving Duckbill	20-22
72 Crooked Crow	15-20
73 Frenzied Flamingo	10-12
74 Fleet-Footed Antelope	15-20
75 Pugnacious Penguin	18-22
76 Ossified Orangutan	10-12

Laser Beasts

77 Blue Eagle	18-20
78 Spark Shark	18-20
79 Sailon	18-20
80 Shrew	18-20
81 Tigerburn	18-20
82 Condorassian	18-20
83 Groundwolf	18-20

84 Fly Sailor	18-20	
85 Zariganian	18-20	
86 Rainbow Sam	18-20	
87 Shool	18-20	
88 Brain Mouse	18-20	
89 Brown Lion	85-90	
90 Grencats	50-55	
91 Fight Horn	65-70	
92 Hustlebear	70-75	
93 Battle Fennec	70-75	
94 Killer Hound	55-60	
95 Dragon Seahorn	85-90	
96 Strong Hurricane	50-55	
97 Sea Panic	70-75	
98 Puzzlecolor	110+	
99 Mantfrenzy	60-65	
100 Scopecougar	95-100	
101 Skull Grotese	210-220+	
102 Kingbuster	240-250+	
103 Slag King	50+	
104 Howler/Jeerer Monkey	60-65+	
105 Hornhead	175-185+	
106 Monkey Fighter	60-65+	
107 Flying Dragon	185-195+	
108 Kickback	215-225+	
109 Skybat	40-45+	
110 Grin Reefer	215-225+	
111 Salmomanther	225-230+	
112 Dino Gator	45-50+	

Battle Chariots

Battling Big Horn	10-12	35-40 (55-65+ MISB)
Deer Staker	10-12	35-40 (55-65+ MISB)
Tearin Tiger	10-12	35-40 (55-65+ MISB)

Battle Sleds

Buzzsaw with Dino Gator	20-25	40 (75+ MISB)
Eagle with Skybat	20-25	40 (75+ MISB)
Svannah with Sky King	20-25	40 (75+ MISB)

Transports (playsets)

Blazing Eagle	40-45	65-70 (85+ MISB)
Shocking Shark	30-35	55 (75+ MISB)
Wood Beetle	35-40	55-60 (75-80+ MISB)

Buck Rogers in the 25th Century
(Mego, 1979)

Figures, 3-3/4"

Princess Ardella	6	50
Buck Rogers	15-20	60
Draco	6	20
Draconian Guard	10	20
Doctor Huer	6	20
Killer Kane	6	15
Tiger Man	10	25
Twiki	20	45
Wilma Deering	12	15

12" figures

Buck Rogers	30	75
Doctor Huer	30	65
Draco	30	60
Draconian Guard	30	75
Killer Kane	30	80
Tiger Man	30	125
Twiki ("Walking")	30	60

Vehicles and Accessories

Draconian Marauder	25	50
Land Rover	20	40

Laserscope Fighter	20	40
Star Fighter	25	50
Star Fighter Command Center playset	40-50	75-80 (110-125+ MISB)
Star Searcher	30	60

Captain Action
(Ideal, 1966-67)

The year released is *after* the item description.

12" figures

Captain Action, 1966 (with red-shirted Lone Ranger on box)	200	500
Captain Action, 1966 (with blue-shirted Lone Ranger on box)	200	500
Captain Action, 1967 (with parachute offer on box)	275	700
Captain Action (photo box)	250	450
Dr. Evil, 1967 (photo box)	250	450
Dr. Evil, Lab Set - Display Box (all Dr. Evil accessories)	1000	3000
Dr. Evil, Lab Set - Mailer Box (mailer version of above)	1000	2500

9" figures

Action Boy, 1967	275	900
Action Boy, 1968 (with space suit)	350	1100

Action Boy Costumes

Aqualad, 1967	300	900
Robin, 1967	300	1200
Superboy, 1967	300	1000

Captain Action Costumes

Aquaman, 1966	160	600
Aquaman, 1967 (with flasher ring)	180	950
Batman, 1966	225	700

Captain Action, Flash Gordon outfit, Ideal, 1967, $600 MIB.

Batman, 1967 (with flasher ring)	250	1100
Buck Rogers, 1967	450	2700
Captain America, 1966	220	900
Captain America, 1967 (with flasher ring)	225	1200
Flash Gordon, 1966	200	600
Flash Gordon, 1967 (with flasher ring)	225	800
Green Hornet, 1967	2000	7500
Lone Ranger, 1966 (red shirt)	200	700
Lone Ranger, 1967 (blue shirt, with flasher ring)	500	1000
Phantom, 1966	225	775
Phantom, 1967(with flasher ring)	250	900
Sgt. Fury, 1966	200	800
Spider-Man, 1967	550	8000
Steve Canyon, 1966	200	700
Steve Canyon, 1967 (with flasher ring)	200	700
Superman, 1966	200	700
Superman, 1967 (with flasher ring)	225	1100
Tonto, 1967	375	1100

Playsets and Accessory Sets

Action Cave Carrying Case, 1967	400	700
Directional Communicator Set, 1966	110	300
Dr. Evil Sanctuary, 1967	2500	3500
Jet Mortar, 1966	110	300
Parachute Pack, 1966	100	225
Power Pack, 1966	125	250
Quick Change Chamber, 1967	750	900
Silver Streak Amphibian, 1967	800	1200
Silver Streak Garage, 1966-1968	1500	2000
Survival Kit, 1967	125	275
Vinyl Headquarters Carrying Case, 1967	200	500
Weapons Arsenal, 1966	110	225

Captain Action reissue, Playing Mantis, 1998, $25 MIB.

Captain Action Dr. Evil, reissue, Playing Mantis, 1998, $30 MIB.

Captain Action Lone Ranger, reissue, Playing Mantis, 1998, $30 MIB.

Captain Action Green Hornet, reissue, Playing Mantis, 1998, $20 MIB.

Captain Action Flash Gordon, reissue, Playing Mantis, 1998, $25 MIB.

Captain Action, Reissues
(Playing Mantis, 1998-99)

12" figures and outfits

Captain Action (small box; Diamond exclusive)	10-12	25-30
Captain Action (deluxe box)	10-12	22-25
Dr. Evil (small box; Diamond exclusive)	10-12	30-35
Dr. Evil (deluxe box)	10-12	25-30
Flash Gordon	12-15	25
Green Hornet Outfit (Diamond exclusive)	12-15	25-30
Green Hornet (Kay-Bee exclusive)	8-10	20
Kabai Singh (outfit, Diamond exclusive)	12-15	25-30
Kato (outfit)	12-15	25-30
Kato (Kay-Bee exclusive)	8-10	20
Kid Action (Diamond exclusive)	15-20+	40-45+
Lone Ranger	8-10	20
Lone Ranger (red costume set)	8-10	25-30
Lone Ranger (blue costume, Diamond exclusive)	12-15	25-30
Ming the Merciless	12-15	25
Phantom, The (outfit, Diamond exclusive)	12-15	25-30
Tonto	8-10	20

Comic Action Heroes
(Mego, 1975-78)

Aquaman	30	75
Batman	20	75
Captain America	20	75
Green Goblin	22	125
Hulk	20	50
Joker	20	75
Penguin	20	75
Robin	20	65
Shazam!	20	75
Spider-Man	20	75

Comic Heroine Posin' Dolls, Batgirl, Ideal, 1967, $5,500 MIB.

Superman	20	65
Wonder Woman	20	65

Vehicles and Accessories

Batcopter with Batman	50	100
Batmobile with Batman and Robin	75	150
Collapsing Tower with Invisible Plane and Wonder Woman	100	200
Exploding Bridge with Batmobile	100	200
Fortress of Solitude with Superman	100	200
Mangler	125	300
Spidercar with Spider-Man and Green Goblin	100	300

Comic Heroine Posin' Dolls
(Ideal, 1967)

Batgirl	1500	5500
Mera	1000	4500
Supergirl	1000	4500
Wonder Woman	1000	4500

DC Comics Super Heroes
(Toy Biz, 1989)

As these were some of Toy Biz's first action figure offerings, they had interestingly low quality sculpts, posability and accessories. However, Toy Biz would grow to dominate the action figure aisle of retail stores from 2002-present with Marvel Legends and other Marvel Comics super hero toys.

Aquaman	5	10
Batman	3	10
Bob the Goon	5	10
Flash	4	10
Flash (second version, with Turbo Platform)	5	10
Green Lantern	8	20
Hawkman	8	20
Joker	4	10
Lex Luthor	3	8

DC Comics Super Heroes Mr. Freeze, Toy Biz, 1989, $10 MIP.

DC Comics Super Heroes Riddler, Toy Biz, 1989, $8 MIP.

Red Tornado, DC Direct, 1998, $15 MIP.

Mr. Freeze	4	10
Penguin (long missile)	8	20
Penguin (short missile)	8	30
Penguin (umbrella-firing)	3	8
Riddler	4	8
Superman	8-10	30
Two-Face	8-10	18-20
Wonder Woman	6-8	12-15

DC Direct

(1998-present; comic and specialty store exclusives)

Assorted

Eclipso	6	10
Enemy Ace (deluxe box)	10-12	25-30
Golden Age Sandman	6-8	10
Golden Age Sandman (variant)	6-8	10
Lobo with Cycle and Dawg (deluxe boxed)	15	30-32
Martian Manhunter	10-12	20-22
Metamorpho (deluxe box)	12-15	30-35
Red Tornado	6-8	12-15
Sgt. Rock	6-8	12-15
Modern Age Starman	8-10	15
Modern Age Starman (variant)	8-10	16-18
Swamp Thing	20-25	55-60
Swamp Thing (variant)	18-20	45-50
Phantom Stranger	8-10	18-20
Plastic Man	6-8	12-15
Plastic Man (variant)	6-8	16-18
Wonder Woman	10	20-22
Wonder woman (variant)	12-15	25-30

Amazing Androids

Amazo	6	10
Hourman	6	10
Tomorrow Woman	6	10

Batman The Long Halloween: The Joker, DC Direct, $13 MIP.

Artist Signature Series: Hush

Batman (by Jim Lee)	40+	85-95

Artist Signature Series: Kingdom Come

Superman (by Alex Ross)	40+	85-95

Authority, The

Apollo	5	10
Engineer The	5	10
Jenny Sparks	5	10
Midnighter	5	10

Batman: Dark Knight Returns, The

Batman	10-12	22-24
Joker, The	8-10	14-18
Robin (Carrie Kelly)	8-10	14-18
Superman	10-12	22-24

Batman: Hush

Series 1

Batman	8-12	18-20
Huntress	8-10	14-18
Hush	8-10	14-18
Joker	8-10	14-18
Poison Ivy	8-10	14-18

Mail-away

Jason Todd (Toyfare exclusive)	25-30	65-70

Series 2

Catwoman	8-12	18-20
Hush	12-14	22-25
Nightwing	12-14	22-25
Riddler, The	8-10	14-18
Superman	8-10	14-18

Batman The Long Halloween: Mad Hatter, DC Direct, $13 MIP.

Series 3

Alfred Pennyworth	8-10	14-18
Commissioner Gordon	8-10	14-18
R'as Al Ghul	8-10	14-18
Scarecrow	8-10	14-18
Stealth Jumper Batman	6-8	12-14

Batman: Imported Japanese figures, by Yamoto

Series 1

Batman	6-8	14-16
Harley Quinn	6-8	14-16
Joker, The	6-8	14-16
Robin	6-8	14-16

Series 2

Batman	6-8	14-16
Penguin	6-8	14-16
Poison Ivy	6-8	14-16
Riddler	6-8	14-16

Batman: Imported Japanese figures, by Kia Asamiya

Series 3

Batman	6-8	14-16
Catwoman	6-8	14-16
Joker, The	6-8	14-16
Two-Face, The	6-8	14-16

Batman: The Long Halloween

Batman	4-6	11-13
Catwoman	6-8	12-16
Joker	4-6	11-13
Mad Hatter	4-6	11-13
Two-Face	4-6	11-13

Classic Crime Syndicate

Johnny Quick	4-6	10-12

Classic Heroes: The Question, DC Direct, $20 MIP.

Owlman	4-6	10-12
Power Ring	4-6	10-12
Superwoman	4-6	10-12
Ultraman	4-6	10-12

Classic Heroes

Blue Beetle	30-35	65-70
Phantom Lady	10-12	18-20
Question, The	10-12	18-20
Uncle Sam	8	12-15

Crisis on Infinite Earths

Harbinger	4-6	10-12
Monitor	4-6	10-12
Psycho Pirate	4-6	10-12
Robin	4-6	10-12
Supergirl	4-6	10-12

DC Speedsters

Impulse	4-6	10-12
Kid Flash	4-6	10-12
Max Mercury	4-6	10-12

First Appearance

Series 1

Batman	6-8	12-14
Flash	4-6	10-12
Shazam!	4-6	10-12
Wonder Woman	4-6	10-12

Series 2

Green Lantern	4-6	10-12
Hawkman	4-6	10-12
Robin	4-6	10-12
Superman	4-6	10-12

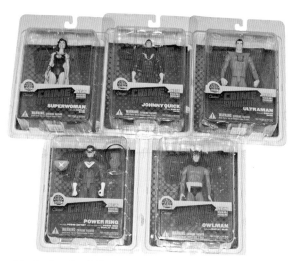

Crime Syndicate from DC Direct. Top row left to right: Superwoman, Johnny Quick, Ultraman. Bottom row left to right: Power Ring, Owlman. Each figure is worth $12 MIP.

Series 3

Batgirl	8-10	14-18
Composite Superman	6	10-12
Nightwing	8-10	14-18
Riddler	6	10-12

Flash Rogues Gallery

Captain Cold	10-12	18-24
Gorilla Grodd (deluxe boxed)	15-18	30-35
Mirror Master	7-9	11-13

Green Lantern

Series 1

Sinestro	6	10-12
Star Sapphire	6	12-14

Series 2

John Stewart	10-12	20-22
Tomar Re	6	10

Series 3

Green Lantern (new series)

Black Hand	6	10-12
Ganthet and Guardian	6	10-12
Hal Jordan	6	12-16
Kilowog	10-12	16-20
Parallax	8	12-14

Mail-away

Emerald Shield Green Lantern (Wizard magazine)	5	12-16

Green Lantern Corps

Effigy	6	10-12
Green Lantern: Guy Gardner	18-22	38-45
Silver Age Green Lantern	10-12	15-18

JLA Adam Strange, Series 2, DC Direct, $10 MIP.

JLA Enlongated Man, Series 2, DC Direct, $10 MIP.

Hard-Travelling Heroes

Black Canary	8-10	18-22
Green Arrow	18-22	30-35
Green Lantern: Hal Jordan	22-24	38-42

Just-Us-League of Stupid Heroes

Alfred E. Newman as Batman	6-8	15-20
Alfred E. Newman as Flash	3-4	10-12
Alfred E. Newman as Green Arrow	3-4	10-12
Alfred E. Newman as Green Lantern	3-4	10-12
Alfred E. Newman as Robin	3-4	10-12
Alfred E. Newman as Superman	6-8	15-20

JLA

Series 1

Aquaman	6-8	12-16
Flash	6-8	14-18
Green Lantern	6-8	12-16
Superman	10-12	18-20
Wonder Woman	8-10	15-18

Series 2

Adam Strange, The	5	10
Atom, The	5	10
Elongated Man, The	5	10
Firestorm, The	5	10

Justice/JLA (Alex Ross)

Series 1

Bizarro	4-6	10-12
Cheetah	4-6	10-12
Flash	6	12-14
Sinestro	4-6	10
Superman	8-10	14-16
Superman (chase variant)	25-28	65-70+

Justice: Flash, Series 1, DC Direct, $14 MIP.

Justice: Superman, Series 1, DC Direct, $16 MIP.

1st Appearance Golden Age Green Lantern, DC Direct, $26 MIP.

Series 2

Aquaman	4-6	10-12
Batman	4-6	10-12
Black Canary	4-6	10-12
Black Manta	4-6	10-12
Parasite	4	10

JSA

Series 1

Golden Age Flash	15-17	22-26
Golden Age Green Lantern	15-17	22-26
Golden Age Starman	15-17	22-26
Golden Age Wonder Woman	15-17	22-26

Series 2

Golden Age Dr. Mid-Nite	15-18	25-30
Golden Age Hourman	10-12	20-22

Series 3

Power Girl	28-35	65-75
Solomon Grundy		
(deluxe box with bonus Pocket Super Hero)	15	30-35
Wildcat	15-18	25-30

Series 4

Shade, The	4-6	10-12
Vandal Savage	4	10

Kingdom Come

Series 1

Green Lantern	10-12	20-22
Hawkman	8-10	15
Superman	13-15	25-30
Wonder Woman	10-12	25-30

Exclusive

Red Arrow (Wizard magazine)	38-45	n/a

Series 2

Batman	12-15	25-30
Kid Flash	8-10	13-15
Red Robin	8-10	12-14
Shazam!	10-12	25-30

Series 3

Deadman	4	10
Flash, The	4	10
Magog	4	10
Wonder Woman, in armor	8	14

Legion of Super-Heroes

Series 1

Cosmic Boy	4-6	8-10
Lightning Lad	4-6	8-10
Saturn Girl	4-6	8-10

Series 2

Brainiac 5	4-6	8-10
Mon-El	4-6	8-10
Mordru	4-6	8-10

Series 3

Chameleon Boy	4-6	8-10
Star Boy	4-6	8-10
Sun Boy	4-6	8-10
Ultra Boy	4-6	8-10

Series 4

Colossal Boy	4-6	8-10
Ferro-Lad	4-6	8-10
Invisible Kid	4-6	8-10
Timberwolf	4-6	8-10

Mages, Mystics & Magicians: Zatanna, DC Direct, $10 MIP.

Mad Magazine

Alfred E. Newman	12	24-26
Black Spy	12	24-26
White Spy	12	24-26
Mad 50th Anniversary Box Set		
(Alfred E. Newman and Spy vs. Spy)	14-16	25-32

Mystics, Mages and Magicians

Dr. Fate	10-12	25-28
John Costantine	4	10-12
Spectre: Jim Corrigan	6-8	12-16
Zatanna	4	8-10

Other Worlds

Deadman	4	10
Demon, The	4-6	10-12
Spectre, The (Hal Jordan)	4	10

Planetary

Drummer, The	5	10
Elijah Snow	5	10
Jakita Wagner	5	10

Preacher

Cassidy	4-5	8-10
Jesse Custer	4-5	8-10
Jesse Custer	4-5	8-10
Jesse Custer (variant, white suit)	8	14-16
Tulip	4-5	8-10
Saint of Killers	4-5	8-10

Sandman

Daniel	4-5	10-12
Delirium	4-5	10-12
Desire	4-5	10-12
Sandman: Morpheus	4-5	10-12
Sandman: Morpheus (variant)	6-8	12-15

Smallville: Lex Luthor, Clark Kent, Lana Lang, DC Direct, $17 MIP each.

Wonder Woman Allies and Villains

Ares	4-6	10
Artemis	4-6	10
Cheetah	6-8	10-12

Boxed Sets

Aquaman and Aqualad Two Pack (Aquaman and Aqualad)	20-22	40-45
Birds of Prey (Black Canary, Huntress, and Oracle)	14-18	30-34
Brave and The Bold #28 Gift Set	18-20	38-40
Classic Teen Titans Box Set	10-12	22-24
Hawkman and Hawkgirl	20-22	65-70
New Gods (Big Barda, Mr. Miracle, and Oberon)	12-15	22-25
New Gods (Darkseid and Orion)	20-24	40-45
Promethea and Sophie	6-8	12-15
Sandman: Incarnations (Sandman: Dream Hunters, Sandman: Arabian Nights)	10	20
Shazam! (Captain Marvel and Billy Batson)	12-15	22-27
Silver Age Batgirl and Joker Set	12-14	22-26
Silver Age Batman and Robin Set	12-14	22-24
Silver Age Batwoman and Batgirl	10-12	20-22
Silver Age Catwoman and The Penguin	18-20	35-40
Silver Age Flash and Kid Flash	18-20	35-40
Silver Age Green Arrow and Speedy	15-18	32-35
Silver Age Superboy and Supergirl	12-14	22-25
Silver Age Superman and Lois Lane	12-14	22-25
Silver Age Wonder Woman and Wonder Girl	12-14	22-25
Tom Strong and Pneuman	6-8	12-15

Dungeons and Dragons

(LJN, 1983)

Series 1 (1983)

Figures, 3-4"

Fantastic Four: Human Torch, spark action and glow-in-the-dark variations, Toy Biz, 1995, $10 MIP for spark action, $15 MIP for glow-in-the-dark.

Drex	55	120
Elkhorn	20	50
Grimsword	30	70
Hawkler	50	100
Strongheart	20	45
Warduke	20	45
Zarak	20	45
Zorgar	50	120

Figures, 5-6"; with new feature: "Shield-Shooting Action"

Mandoom	60	120
Metta Flame	60	120
Northlord	50	100
Ogre King	65	130
Young Male Titan	50	100

Fantastic Four
(Toy Biz, 1995)

Series 1 (1995)

Black Bolt	5-6	15
Dr. Doom	3-4	8-10
Mr. Fantastic	5-6	12-15
Mole Man	3-4	8
Silver Surfer	3-4	8-10
Terrax	3-4	8
Thing, The	3-4	8

Series 2 (1995)

Blastaar	3-4	8
Dragon Man	3-4	8
Firelord	5-6	10-12
Gorgon	3-4	8

Ghostbusters, The Real
(Kenner, 1986-90)

Series 1 (1986)

Prices are for figures with all accessories and ghosts

Egon with Gulper Ghost	15-20	60-70
Peter with Grabber Ghost	15-20	60-70
Ray with Wrapper Ghost	15-20	60-70
Winston with Chomper Ghost	15-20	60-70

Creatures

Green Ghost (Note: not called "Slimer")	20	50-55
Stay-Puft Marshmallow Man	45	75-80

Vehicles and Accessories

Ecto-1	35	60-65 (90-110+ MISB)
Ghost Zapper	5-10	15-20

Series 2 (1987)

Bad to the Bone Ghost	5	15
Banshee Bomber (Gooper Ghost)	15	35-40+
Bug-Eye Ghost	5	15
H2 Ghost	5	15
Sludge Bucket (Gooper Ghost)	15	35-40+
Squisher (Gooper Ghost)	15	35-40+

Vehicles and Accessories

Firehouse playset	45-55	70-75 (170-180+ MISB)
Ghostpopper	15-20	35-40 (50+ MISB)
Proton Pack	18-25	45 (100+ MISB)

Series 3 (1988)

Fright Features, Heroes

Egon Spengler	8-10	25-30
Janine Melnitz	8-10	25-30
Peter Venkman	8-10	25-30

Ray Stantz	8-10	25-30
Winston Zeddmore	8-10	25-30

Ghosts

Gooper Green Ghost	12	25-35+
Granny Gross	5-10	15-20
Hard Hat Horror	5-10	15-20
Mail Fraud	5-10	15-20
Mini Goopers	5-10	12-15
Mini Traps	5-10	12-15
Mini Shooter	5-10	12-15
Pull Speed Ahead Ghost	5-10	15-20
Terror Trash	5-10	15-20
Tombstone Tackle	5-10	15-20
X-Cop	5-10	15-20

Vehicles and Accessories

Airsickness	10-12	25-30
Highway Haunter (Haunted Vehicle)	10-12	25-30
Ecto-2	12-16	25-30 (35+ MISB)
Ghost Spooker	12-15	20-25
Ectoplasm	3-4	6-10
Wicked Wheelie (Haunted Vehicle)	10-12	25-30

Series 4 (1989)

Scream'n Heroes

Egon Spengler	10-12	25-30
Janine Melnitz	10-12	25-30
Peter Vekman	10-12	25-30
Ray Stantz	10-12	25-30
Winston Zeddmore	10-12	25-30

Super Fright Features

Egon Spengler	12-14	27-32
Janine Melnitz	12-14	27-32

Peter Vekman	12-14	27-32
Ray Stantz	12-14	27-32
Winston Zeddmore	12-14	27-32

Ghosts

Dracula	12-14	27-32
Fearsome Flush	10-12	22-25
Frankenstein	12-14	27-32
Hunchback	12-14	27-32
Mummy	12-14	27-32
Wolfman	12-14	27-32
Slimer with Proton Pack	12-14	35-40
Zombie	12-14	27-32

Vehicles and Accessories

Ecto-Popper and Ecto-Goggles	15-20	25-30
Ecto-500	12-15	25-30
Ecto-3	12-15	25-30
Ghost Trap	20-25+	35-40 (60-65+ MISB)
Water Zapper	12-15	20-25

Series 5 (1990)

Power Pack Heroes

Egon Spengler	10-12	20-22
Janine Melnitz	10-12	20-22
Louis Tully	10-12	20-22
Peter Vekman	10-12	20-22
Ray Stantz	10-12	20-22
Winston Zeddmore	10-12	20-22

Slimed Heroes

Egon Spengler	8-10	15-18
Louis Tully	8-10	15-18
Peter Vekman	8-10	15-18
Ray Stantz	8-10	15-18
Winston Zeddmore	8-10	15-18

Gobblin' Goblins

Nasty Neck	12-15	25-30
Terrible Teeth	12-15	25-30
Terror Tongue	12-15	25-30

Vehicles and Accessories

Ecto-1A	20-25	45-50 (65-75+ MISB)
Ecto-Blaster	10-12	25-30
Ecto-Bomber	15-20	30-35
Ghost Nabber	18-22	35-40
Ghost Sweeper	10-12	22-25

Series 6 (1991)

Ecto-Glow Heroes

Egon Spengler	12-15	25-30
Louis Tully	12-15	25-30
Peter Vekman	12-15	25-30
Ray Stantz	12-15	25-30
Winston Zeddmore	12-15	25-30

G.I. Joe, 12"

(Hasbro, 1964-68)

Note: These are arranged by the type of the four standard G.I. Joe soldiers—Action Marine, Action Pilot, Action Sailor, and Action Soldier.

Action Marine

Figures and Figure Sets

Action Marine	125	145	450
Marine Medic Series	325	425	1550
Talking Action Marine	175	200	850

Uniform/Equipment Sets

Beachhead Assault Field Pack Set	100	175	325
Beachhead Assault Tent Set	100	200	425
Communications Flag Set	200	250	475

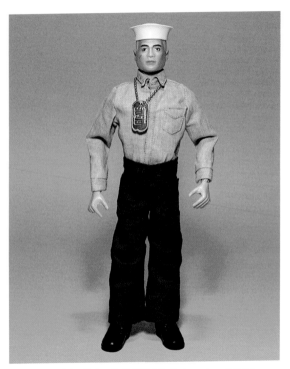

G.I. Joe Action Sailor, Hasbro, 1964, $450 MIB. Photo courtesy of Vincent Santelmo.

Dress Uniform Set	225	550	1650
Fighter Pilot Set	400	650	1550
Scramble Communications Set	35	75	175
Scramble Set	125	225	950
Survival Life Rat Set	75	125	550

Vehicle Sets

Crash Crew Fire Truck Set	950	1700	3500
Official Space Capsule Set	175	225	350
Official Space Capsule Set with Flotation	200	325	700
Spacewalk Mystery	120	265	450

Action Sailor

Figures and Figure Sets

Action Sailor	125	225	450
Navy Scuba Set	300	450	3250
Talking Action Sailor	200	330	1250
Talking Landing Signal Officer Set	325	350	3500
Talking Shore Patrol Set	200	450	3500

Uniform/Equipment Sets

Annapolis Cadet	275	375	1350
Breeches Buoy	325	425	1500
Deep Freeze	250	375	1600
Deep Sea Diver Set	325	425	1850
Frogman Underwater Demolition Set	175	250	1500
Landing Signal Officer	225	350	575
Navy Attack Helmet Set	35	75	150
Navy Attack Set	60	125	425
Navy Basics Set	25	55	125
Navy Dress Parade Set	45	80	175
Navy L.S.O. Equipment Set	40	80	150
Navy Life Ring Set	25	45	150
Navy Machine Gun Set	40	80	175
Sea Rescue Set	95	135	500
Shore Patrol	500	1000	2000

Combat Demolition Set	65	100	525
Combat Engineer Set	125	175	625
Combat Fatigue Pants Set	15	25	110
Combat Fatigue Shirt Set	20	30	125
Combat Field Jacket Set	65	100	525
Combat Field Pack Deluxe Set	75	125	325
Combat Helmet Set	20	35	75
Combat Mess Set	20	45	85
Combat Rifle Set	55	100	325
Combat Sandbags Set	10	40	85
Command Post Poncho Set	85	125	400
Command Post Small Arms Set	30	60	100
Dress Parade Adventure Pack	750	1250	3500
Green Beret and Small Arms Set	85	110	350
Green Beret Machine Gun Outpost Set			
(Sears exclusive)	225	450	1500
Heavy Weapons Set	175	325	1750
Military Police Uniform Set	450	1650	3000
Mountain Troops Set	90	175	350
Sabotage Set	125	250	1800
Ski Patrol Deluxe Set	170	350	1250
Ski Patrol Helmet and Small Arms Set	35	75	135
Snow Troop Set	20	45	175
Special Forces Bazooka Set	35	45	225
Special Forces Uniform Set	200	375	1000
West Point Cadet Uniform Set	250	475	1500

Vehicle Sets

Amphibious Duck	175	375	700
Armored Car	150	300	500
Helicopter	150	300	500
Jet Fighter Plane	225	475	800
Military Staff Car	200	400	750
Motorcycle and Sidecar	75	150	325

Official Combat Jeep Set	200	375	550
Personnel Carrier/Mine Sweeper	300	350	700

G.I. Joe, Action Soldiers of the World
(Hasbro, 1966, 12" figures)

Figures and Figure Sets

Australian Jungle Fighter (figure and full accessory set)	250	400	2500
Australian Jungle Fighter (standard set, no accessories)	150	275	1200
British Commando (figure and full accessory set)	300	425	2500
British Commando (standard set, no accessories)	150	275	1750
Foreign Soldiers of the World (talking adventure pack)	750	825	5000
French Resistance Fighter (figure and full accessory set)	200	250	2250
French Resistance Fighter (standard set, no accessories)	125	225	1250
German Storm Trooper (figure and full accessory set)	275	425	2500
German Storm Trooper (standard set, no accessories)	275	325	1300
Japanese Imperial Soldier (figure and full accessory set)	425	675	2700
Japanese Imperial Soldier (standard set, no accessories)	300	325	1425
Russian Infantry Man (figure and full accessory set)	315	425	2250
Russian Infantry Man (standard set, no accessories)	275	400	1250
Uniforms of Six Nations	750	950	2500

G.I. Joe Black Adventurer, Hasbro, 1970-73, $375 MIB. Photo courtesy of Vincent Santelmo.

Uniform/Equipment Sets

Australian Jungle Fighter Set	25	50	250
British Commando Set	125	200	325
French Resistance Fighter Set	25	50	275
German Storm Trooper Set	125	175	325
Japanese Imperial Soldier Set	175	275	625
Russian Infantry Man Set	175	220	325

G.I. Joe, Adventure Team
(Hasbro, 1970-76)

Figures and Figure Sets

Air Adventurer (1970)	120	375	400
Air Adventurer (1974, with Kung-Fu Grip)	95	160	325
Air Adventurer (1976, "Life-Like Body")	75	100	200
Black Adventurer (1970)	125	150	375
Black Adventurer (1976, with "Life-Like Body" and "Kung-Fu Grip")	85	125	225
Bulletman	60	100	175
Eagle-Eye Black Commando	85	125	250
Eagle-Eye Land Commander	65	80	150
Eagle-Eye Man of Action	65	80	165
Intruder Commander (enemy)	50	60	135
Intruder Warrior (enemy)	50	60	175
Land Adventurer (1970)	45	90	160
Land Adventurer (1976, with "Life-Like Body" and "Kung-Fu Grip" and uniform set)	50	65	200
Land Adventurer (1976)	20	50	180
Man of Action (1970)	50	75	225
Man of Action (1976, with "Life-Like Body" and "Kung-Fu Grip")	45	75	200
Mike Powers, Atomic Man	20	45	125
Sea Adventurer (1970)	45	95	250

Sea Adventurer (1974, with "Life-Like Body" and "Kung-Fu Grip")	55	135	295
Sea Adventurer (1976)	50	80	225
Secret Mountain Outpost	50	85	200
Talking Adventure Team Black Commander 1974, with "Kung-Fu Grip")	85	350	750
Talking Adventure Team Commander (1970, with "Life-Like" hair and beard)	65	140	400
Talking Adventure Team Commander (with "Kung-Fu Grip")	75	200	500
Talking Astronaut	90	175	430
Talking Black Commander	125	300	600
Talking Commander	75	115	500
Talking Man of Action	75	200	650

Uniform/Equipment Sets

Adventure Team Headquarters Set	50	125	300
Adventure Team Training Center Set	75	125	225
Aerial Reconnaissance Set	75	125	242
Attack at Vulture Falls	75	150	275
Black Widow Rendezvous	125	200	350
Buried Bounty	10	25	85
Capture of the Pygmy Gorilla Set	100	175	485
Challenge of Savage River	100	175	350
Chest Winch Set	10	15	65
Command Para Drop	175	250	550
Copter Rescue Set	15	20	30
Danger of the Depths Set	100	175	325
Danger Ray Detection	45	90	225
Dangerous Climb Set	20	35	75
Dangerous Mission Set	20	35	75
Demolition Set	75	100	250
Desert Explorer Set	20	40	80
Desert Survival Set	20	40	80

Dive to Danger	150	250	450
Diver's Distress	35	70	125
Drag Bike Set	25	65	125
Eight Ropes of Danger Set	125	225	375
Emergency Rescue Set	45	75	145
Equipment Tester Set	15	75	140
Escape Car Set	30	60	85
Escape Slide Set	15	25	40
Fangs of the Cobra	125	175	235
Fantastic Freefall Set	125	200	345
Fight for Survival Set	20	30	70
Fire Fighter Set	20	30	55
Flying Rescue Set	35	60	85
Flying Space Adventure Set	400	600	3700
Footlocker	35	45	200
Green Danger	30	75	60
Hidden Missile Discovery Set	100	225	1750
Hidden Treasure Set	15	25	40
High Voltage Escape Set	40	75	110
Hurricane Spotter Set	55	110	220
Jaws of Death	325	500	650
Jettison to Safety	85	200	275
Jungle Ordeal Set	15	25	65
Jungle Survival Set	15	60	180
Karate Set	35	70	210
Laser Rescue Set	20	35	45
Life-Line Catapult Set	15	25	85
Long Range Recon	10	20	35
Magnetic Flaw Detector Set	10	20	55
Mine Shaft Breakout	70	125	250
Missile Recovery Set	100	200	325
Mystery of the Boiling Lagoon	150	200	295
Night Surveillance	65	160	265

Peril of the Raging Inferno	85	150	275
Photo Reconnaissance Set	20	30	65
Race for Recovery	20	35	140
Radiation Detection Set	30	50	160
Raging River Dam-Up	100	225	450
Rescue Raft Set	15	45	65
Revenge of the Spy Shark	50	175	400
Rock Blaster	10	20	35
Rocket Pack Set	10	20	75
Sample Analyzer Set	45	145	255
Search for the Abominable Snowman Set	110	175	290
Secret Agent Set	30	55	190
Secret Courier	45	80	135
Secret Mission Set	45	65	135
Secret Mission to Spy Island Set	75	175	400
Secret Rendezvous Set	10	20	35
Seismograph Set	10	20	35
Shocking Escape	125	240	525
Signal Flasher Set	20	30	65
Sky Dive to Danger	90	150	350
Solar Communicator Set	10	20	35
Sonic Rock Blaster Set	10	20	35
Special Assignment	30	55	135
Thermal Terrain Scanner Set	25	35	50
Three-in-One Super Adventure Set ("#1"; Cold of the Arctic, Heat of the Desert, and Danger of the Jungle)	250	400	750
Three-in-One Super Adventure Set ("#2"; Danger of the Depths, Secret Mission to Spy Island, and Flying Space Adventure)	550	975	1250
Thrust Into Danger	45	55	175
Trouble at Vulture Pass	75	175	325
Turbo Copter Set	15	35	65

Undercover Agent Set	15	30	45
Underwater Demolition Set	15	20	55
Underwater Explorer Set	15	30	60
Volcano Jumper Set	45	80	250
White Tiger Hunt Set	80	180	340
Windboat Set	10	25	65
Winter Rescue Set	40	75	150

Vehicle Sets

Action Sea Sled	25	40	85
Adventure Team Vehicle Set	50	75	225
All Terrain Vehicle	50	75	125
Amphicat	35	55	125
Avenger Pursuit Craft	100	175	275
Big Trapper	75	245	600
Big Trapper Adventure with Intruder	100	150	425
Capture Copter	80	175	325
Capture Copter Adventure with Intruder	110	200	350
Chopper Cycle	30	50	100
Combat Action Jeep	50	65	125
Combat Jeep and Trailer	80	135	550
Devil of the Deep	80	135	325
Fantastic Sea Wolf Submarine	60	100	175
Fate of the Troubleshooter	85	210	310
Giant Air-Sea Helicopter	50	125	225
Helicopter	50	90	150
Mobile Support Vehicle Set	125	200	425
Recovery of the Lost Mummy Adventure	125	250	575
Sandstorm Survival Adventure	125	200	335
Search for the Stolen Idol Set	120	225	400
Secret of the Mummy's Tomb Set	150	600	1500
Shark's Surprise Set with Sea Adventurer	250	375	550
Signal All-Terrain Vehicle	30	65	125
Sky Hawk	65	100	175

G.I. Joe 3-3/4": Flash, Hasbro, 1982, $175 MIP.

Spacewalk Mystery Set with Astronaut	225	300	550
Trapped in the Coils of Doom	250	300	550

G.I. Joe 3-3/4"
(Hasbro, 1982-94)

Series 1 (1982)

Figures, individually packaged

Breaker (straight-armed)	15	125
Cobra (straight-armed)	20-25	250
Cobra Officer (straight-armed)	20-25	250
Flash (straight-armed)	15	175
Grunt (straight-armed)	12-15	125
Rock 'n Roll (straight-armed)	20	175
Scarlett (straight-armed)	20-25	400+
Short-Fuse (straight-armed)	20-22	150
Snake Eyes (straight-armed)	30-35	750+
Stalker (straight-armed)	15-18	200+
Zap (straight-armed, regular bazooka)	15-20	175
Zap (two-handled bazooka)	25-35	325+

Figures, mail-aways

Cobra Commander (straight-armed)	25-30	n/a
Cobra Commander ("Mickey Mouse" Cobra logo)	55-60+	n/a
Major Bludd (swivel-armed)	12-15	n/a

Figures, vehicle drivers

Clutch (straight-armed; VAMP Driver)	10-12	n/a
Grand Slam (straight-armed; Laser Artillery Soldier)	15	n/a
Hawk (straight-armed; Missile Commander)	18-22	n/a
Steeler (straight-armed; Tank Commander)	22-25	n/a

Vehicles, Playsets, and Accessories

FLAK	8-12	25-35 (50+ MISB)

Cobra Missile Command Headquarters (Sears exclusive; sealed, with three

G.I. Joe 3-3/4": Major Bludd, Hasbro, 1983, $300 MIP.

MISB figures: Cobra, Cobra Commander,		
and Cobra Officer)	150-250	500-750 (1100+ MISB)
HAL (with Grand Slam)	15-25	100-125 (250 MISB)
JUMP	12-15	35-45 (80-90 MISB)
MMS (with Hawk)	15-25	100-125 (300+ MISB)
MOBAT (with Steeler)	18-22	150 (325+ MISB)
RAM	10-15	45-50 (85-100 MISB)
VAMP (with Clutch)	25-30	150 (300+ MISB)

Series 2 (1983)

Figures, individually packaged

Airborne	15-20	200+
Breaker (swivel-armed)	15-20	125+
Cobra (swivel-armed)	20-25	250+
Cobra Commander (swivel-armed)	25-30	850+
Cobra Officer (swivel-armed)	20-25	250+
Destro	15-18	300+
Doc	15-18	200+
Flash (swivel-armed)	15-20	175+
Grunt (swivel-armed)	12-15	125+
Gung-Ho	15	250+
Major Bludd	12-15	300+
Rock 'n Roll (swivel-armed)	20	175+
Scarlett (swivel-armed)	20-25	325+
Short-Fuse (swivel-armed, mortar type 3		
[thick-handled])	20-22	150+
Snake-Eyes (swivel-armed)	30-35	450+
Snow Job	15-20	200+
Stalker (swivel-armed)	15-18	200+
Torpedo	12-15	200+
Tripwire	12-15	225+
Zap (swivel-armed)	15-20	175+

G.I. Joe 3-3/4": Torpedo, Hasbro, 1983, $200 MIP.

Figures, vehicle drivers

Ace	10	n/a
Clutch (swivel-armed)	10-12	n/a
Cover Girl	18-22	n/a
Grand Slam ("Silver Pads";		
Laser Jet Pack Soldier)	30-35+	n/a
Hawk (swivel-armed)	18-22	n/a
H.I.S.S. Driver (The Enemy)	15-20	n/a
Steeler (swivel-armed)	22-25	n/a
Viper Pilot (The Enemy; condition is		
based on the Cobra sigil on his chest)	45-75+	n/a
Wild Bill (Helicopter Pilot)	12-15	n/a

Figures, mail-aways

Duke (with American flag sticker)	25-30	
Duke (without sticker)	18-20	

Vehicles, Playsets, and Accessories

APC	18-25	80-100 (200+ MISB)
Battle Gear Accessory Pack #1	10-12	15-20
Cobra F.A.N.G.	20-25	55-60 (125+ MISB)
Cobra H.I.S.S. (with Cobra H.I.S.S. Driver)	22-25	100-125 (275+ MISB)
Collector's Carry Case	12-15	30 (MISP)
Dragonfly XH-1 (with Wild Bill)	25-35	125 (275+ MISB)
Falcon Glider (with "Tan" Grunt)	55	150 (450+ MISB)
G.I. Joe Headquarters Command Center	55-60	90-125 (275-350+ MISB)
JUMP Jet Pack (with "Silver Pads" Grand Slam)	12-15	85-110+ (350+ MISB)
P.A.C. R.A.T.: Flamethrower	5-10	15-20 (35-40 MISB)
P.A.C. R.A.T.: Machine Gun	5-10	15-20 (35-40 MISB)
P.A.C. R.A.T.: Missile Launcher	5-10	15-20 (35-40 MISB)
Pocket Patrol Pack	3-5	15-20 (MOC)
Polar Battle Bear	15-20	50-55 (150+ MISB)
Skystriker XP-14F (with Ace)	55-60	110-125 (275+ MISB)
S.N.A.K.E. Armor (white colored)	15-20	35-45 (85-110+ MISB)

G.I. Joe 3-3/4": Baroness, Hasbro, 1984, $275 MIP.

G.I. Joe 3-3/4": Blowtorch, Hasbro, 1984, $150 MIP.

G.I. Joe 3-3/4": Duke, Hasbro, 1984, $350 MIP.

G.I. Joe 3-3/4": Firefly, Hasbro, 1984, $450 MIP.

G.I. Joe 3-3/4": Mutt and Junkyard, Hasbro, 1984, $250 MIP.

G.I. Joe 3-3/4": Roadblock, Hasbro, 1984, $250 MIP.

G.I. Joe 3-3/4": Airtight, Hasbro, 1985, $100 MIP.

G.I. Joe 3-3/4": Alpine, Hasbro, 1985, $150 MIP.

G.I. Joe 3-3/4": Buzzer, Hasbro, 1985, $100 MIP.

G.I. Joe 3-3/4": Eels, Hasbro, 1985, $190 MIP.

G.I. Joe 3-3/4": Flint, Hasbro, 1985, $140 MIP.

G.I. Joe 3-3/4": Footloose, Hasbro, 1985, $75 MIP.

G.I. Joe 3-3/4": Lady Jaye, Hasbro, 1985, $150 MIP.

G.I. Joe 3-3/4": Quick Kick, Hasbro, 1985, $70 MIP.

G.I. Joe 3-3/4": Snow Serpent, Hasbro, 1985, $100 MIP.

G.I. Joe 3-3/4": Tele-Viper, Hasbro, 1985, $75 MIP.

G.I. Joe 3-3/4": Crimson Guard Commanders Tomax and Xamot, Hasbro, 1985, $180 MIP.

G.I. Joe 3-3/4": Torch, Hasbro, 1985, $100 MIP.

Bivouac	12-15	35 (65-70+ MISB)
Chameleon (with Zartan)	35-45	115 (275-325+ MISB)
Cobra A.S.P.	8-12	30-35 (75-80+ MISB)
Cobra C.L.A.W.	8-12	30-35 (75-80+ MISB)
Hovercraft (Killer W.H.A.L.E., with Cutter)	60-70	100-125 (375+ MISB)
Machine Gun Defense Unit	7-9	15-20 (35-45 MISB)
Missile Defense Unit	7-9	15-20 (35-45 MISB)
Mortar Defense Unit	7-9	15-20 (35-45 MISB)
Mountain Howitzer	12-15	35 (65-70+ MISB)
Night Attack 4-WD Stinger		
(with Cobra Stinger Driver)	25-35	100-110 (300+ MISB)
Rattler (with Wild Weasel)	50-60	125-150 (400+ MISB)
S.H.A.R.C. (with Deep-Six)	18-20	65-75 (175-225+ MISB)
Sky Hawk	10-12	40-45 (110+ MISB)
Slugger (with Thunder)	18-22	75-90 (145-160+ MISB)
VAMP Mark II (with "Tan" Clutch)	18-25	110-130 (300+ MISB)
Watch Tower	12-15	35 (65-70+ MISB)
Water Moccasin (with Copperhead)	18-20	65-70 (110-130+ MISB)

Vehicles, mail-aways

M.A.N.T.A.	8-12	15-20 (MIBaggie)

Series 4 (1985)

Figures, individually packaged

Airtight	10-12	100
Alpine	15-18	125-150+
Barbecue	10-12	125-150+
Bazooka	8-10	100-110
Buzzer	8-12	100+
Crimson Guard	25-30	145-165+
Dusty	12-15	180-200+
Eels	15-18	175-190
Flint	12-15	125-140+
Footloose	12-14	75

Lady Jaye	12-15	135-150+
Quick Kick	7-9	65-70
Ripper	8-10	65
Shipwreck	12-15	90-100+
Snake Eyes	35-40+	350-375+
Snow Serpent	15-20	100+
Tele-Viper	8-10	75
Tomax and Xamot (sold together)	12-18	160-180+
Torch	8-10	95-100

Figures, vehicles drivers

Crankcase (A.W.E. Striker Driver)	6-8	n/a
Frostbite (Snow Cat Driver)	6-8	n/a
Heavy-Metal (Mauler MBT Driver; no microphone)	6-8	n/a
Heavy-Metal (Mauler MBT Driver; with microphone [rarest Joe accessory])	85-110+	
Keel-Haul (Admiral)	12	n/a
Lampreys (Hydrofoil Pilot)	6-8	n/a
Toll-Booth (Bridgelayer Driver)	6-8	n/a

Figures, exclusives

Sgt. Slaughter ("USA" mail-away)	10	20 (MIBaggie)
Tripwire ("Listen 'n Fun" retail exclusive)	30	70-80

Vehicles, Playsets, and Accessories

Air Defense	5	10-15 (20-25 MISB)
Ammo Dump Unit	6-8	10-15 (20-25 MISB)
Armadillo (Mini Tank)	5-7	10 (40 MISB)
A.W.E. Striker (with Crankcase)	18-22	60-65 (110+ MISB)
Battle Gear Accessory Pack #3	6-8	15 (MOC)
Bomb Disposal	5	10-15 (20-25 MISB)
Bridgelayer Toss 'n Cross (with Tollbooth)	15-18	50-55 (125+ MISB)
C.A.T. (Sears exclusive)	85-95	150-165 (375+ MISB)
Check Point Alpha	10-12	15-20 (35+ MISB)

Cobra Bunker	8-10	15 (30+ MISB)
Cobra Ferret	10	25-30 (60-65+ MISB)
Cobra Flight Pod (Trubble Bubble)	18-22	32-38 (65-70+ MISB)
Cobra Rifle Range Unit	10	15-20 (45-50+ MISB)
Forward Observer	8-10	15-18 (35 MISB)
M.B.T. Mauler (with Heavy Metal)		
(no microphone)	70+	125 (400+ MISB)
(with microphone)	175+	225-250 (400+ MISB)
Moray (with Lampreys)		
(with searchlight lens)	85-90	125+ (300+ MISB)
(without lens)	55-60	95-100 (300+ MISB)
Night Landing	10-12	15-20 (50-60+ MISB)
Silver Mirage Motorcycle	15-18	25-30 (50-60+ MISB)
S.M.S. (Sears exclusive)	140-150	225-250 (400+ MISB)
S.N.A.K.E. Armor (blue color)	32-38	50-55 (150-175+ MISB)
Snow Cat (with Frostbite)	20-25	40-45 (125-150+ MISB)
Transportable Tactical Battle Platform	50-60	75-80 (160-175+ MISB)
U.S.S. Flagg (with Keel-Haul)	250-300	600-750 (1100-1300+ MISB)
Weapon Transport	5	10-15 (MISB 20-25)

Vehicles and Accessories, mail-away

Parachute Pack, HALO	5-8	15-20 (mint in sealed baggie)

Series 5 (1986)

Figures, individually packaged

B.A.T.S.	20-25	75-80+
Beach Head	12-15	135-150+
Dial-Tone	10	75-85
Dr. Mindbender	10	60-65
Hawk	10-12	50-60
Iceberg	6	45-50
Leatherneck	12-14	60-65

G.I. Joe 3-3/4": Dr. Mindbender, Hasbro, 1986, $65 MIP.

G.I. Joe 3-3/4": Hawk, Hasbro, 1986, $60 MIP.

G.I. Joe 3-3/4": Lifeline, Hasbro, 1986, $65 MIP.

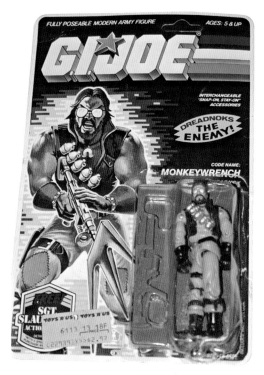

G.I. Joe 3-3/4": Monkeywrench, Hasbro, 1986, $70 MIP.

G.I. Joe 3-3/4": Viper, Hasbro, 1986, $90 MIP.

G.I. Joe 3-3/4": Wet Suit, Hasbro, 1986, $70 MIP.

G.I. Joe 3-3/4": Zarana (with earrings), Hasbro, 1986, $70 MIP.

Lifeline	10-12	60-65
Low Light	10-12	65-70
Mainframe	10-12	60-65
Monkeywrench	10	65-70
Roadblock	10-12	60-65
Sci-Fi	8	45-50
Viper	25	85-90+
Wet-Suit	12-15	65-70+
Zandar	12-15	65
Zarana (with earrings)	13-16	70
Zarana (without earrings)	6-8	45-50

Figures, Mail-aways, and Exclusives

Special Mission: Brazil (Toys 'R Us exclusive; boxed set) MIB 200+ (MISB 375+)

Claymore	22-28	n/a
Dial-Tone	12-15	n/a
Leatherneck	12-15	n/a
Mainframe	12-15	n/a
Wet-Suit	12-15	n/a

Figures, mail-away

The Fridge	8-12	20 (mint in baggie)

Figures, vehicle drivers

A.V.A.C. (Cobra Terror Drome Firebat Pilot)	22-25	n/a
Cross Country (H.A.V.O.C. Driver)	8	n/a
Lift Ticket (Tomahawk Pilot)	16-20	n/a
Motor Viper (Cobra S.T.U.N. Driver)	8	n/a
Serpentor (Cobra Emperor)	14-18	n/a
Sgt. Slaughter (with Triple T)	8	n/a
Slip Stream (Conquest X-30 Pilot)	6-8	n/a
Strato-Viper (Night Raven Pilot)	6-8	n/a
Thrasher (Thunder Machine Driver)	6-8	n/a

Vehicles, Playsets, and Accessories

Air Chariot (with Serpentor)	20-25	50 (100+ MISB)
Battle Gear Accessory Pack #4	6-8	15 (MOC)
Cobra S.T.U.N. (with Motor Viper)	15	30-35 (90+ MISB)
Cobra Surveillance Port	8-10	15-20 (30-35 MISB)
Cobra Terror Drome	150-175	275-300
		(550-575+ MISB)
Terror Drome Firebat (with A.V.A.C.)		
Conquest X-30	22-27	40 (85-90+ MISB)
Devilfish	8-10	25 (40+ MISB)
Dreadnok Air Assualt (Sears exclusive;		
Sky Hawk and Fang)	100-120	250-275 (450+ MISB)
Dreadnok Ground Assault (Sears exclusive;		
4WD and Motorcycle)	110-130	260-280 (475+ MISB)
Dreadnok Swampfire	12-15	25-30 (50+ MISB)
Dreadnok Thunder Machine (with Thrasher)	25-30	45-50 (120+ MISB)
H.A.V.O.C. (with Cross-Country)	18-25	45-50 (175-190+ MISB)
Hydro-Sled	5-6	12-15 (25-30 MISB)
L.A.W.	5-6	12-15 (25-30 MISB)
L.C.V. Recon Sled	5-6	10-12 (20-25 MISB)
Night Raven S3P (with Strato-Viper)	45-50	75-80 (175-200+ MISB)
Outpost Defender	8-10	20 (40+ MISB)
Tomahawk (with Lift-Ticket)	55-60	85+ (250-275+ MISB)
"Triple-T" Tank (with Sgt. Slaughter)	8	25 (75 MISB)

Series 6 (1987)

Figures, individually packaged

Big Boa	10-12	55+
Chuckles	8-10	35
Cobra Commander (with battle armor)	12-15	40-45
Crazylegs	8	25-30
Croc Master	8	25-30
Crystal Ball	6	22-28
Falcon	15-17	65-70

G.I. Joe 3-3/4": Croc Master, Hasbro, 1986, $30 MIP.

G.I. Joe 3-3/4": Jinx, Hasbro, 1986, $55 MIP.

G.I. Joe 3-3/4": Sneak Peek, Hasbro, 1986, $25 MIP.

Fast Draw	12-15	35
Gung-Ho (Marine, Dress Blues)	8	50-55
Jinx	12-15	50-55
Law and Order	12-15	65-70
Outback	18-22	75
Psyche-Out	10	35
Raptor	10	25-30
Sneak Peek	10	25
Techno-Viper	10	25
Tunnel Rat	15-20	55-65

Battle Force 2000

Avalanche (individually carded)	8	20-25
Avalance and Blaster (two-pack)	16	40
Blaster (individually carded)	8	20-25
Blocker (with visor; individually carded)	10-12	20-25
Blocker (without visor; individually carded)	8	20-25
Blocker and Maverick (two-pack)	16	40
Dodger (individually carded)	8	20-25
Dodger and Knockdown (two-pack)	16	40
Knockdown (individually carded)	8	20-25
Maverick (individually carded)	8	20-25

Cobra-La Team

(carded three-pack)	45	65-70
Golobulus	8	n/a
Nemesis Enforcer	15-18	n/a
Royal Guard	14-17	n/a

Sgt. Slaughter's Renegades

(carded three-pack)	25	55+
Mercer	8	n/a
Red Dog	8	n/a
Taurus	8	n/a

Figures, vehicle drivers

Back Stop (Persuader Driver)	8	n/a
Gyro-Viper (Cobra Mamba Pilot)	10-12	n/a
Hard Top (Crawler Driver, with mic)	25-30	n/a
Hard Top (with pistol and microphone)	55-60	n/a
Ice Viper (Ice Snake Driver)	15-20	n/a
Payload (Astronaut)	35-45	n/a
Rumbler (R/C Crossfire Driver)	25	n/a
Sea Slug (Cobra Sea Ray Navigator)	8	n/a
Steam Roller (Mobile Command Center Driver)	15	n/a
W.O.R.M.S. (Cobra Maggot Driver, with antenna)	20-24	n/a
Zanzibar (Dreadnok Pirate)	10-12	n/a

Figures, mail-aways

Starduster	40	90-100 (mint in baggie)
Steel Brigade (regular version)	20-25+	35-40 (mint in baggie)
Steel Brigade (gold helmet)	90-100	120+ (mint in baggie)

Vehicles, Playsets, and Accessories

Air Skiff (with Zanzibar)	5-7	12-15 (40+ MISB)
Battle Gear Accessory Pack #5	6-8	15 (MOC)
Buzz Boar	8-10	12-15 (30+ MISB)
Coastal Defender	6-8	12-15 (25+ MISB)
Cobra Jet Pack	6	12 (20+ MISB)
Crossfire R/C (with Rumbler; "Delta" or "Alpha" models)	25-35	45-50 (125-135+ MISB)
Defiant: Space Vehicle Launch Complex (with Hard Top and Payload)	275-350+	675-750+ (1000+ MISB)
Dreadnok Cycle	8	12 (25-30 MISB)
MAGGOT (with W.O.R.M.S.)	35-40	75 (110 MISB)
Mamba (with Gyro-Viper)	35-40	75 (110 MISB)
Mobile Command Center (with Steam Roller)	45	65-75 (125+ MISB)
Motorized Action Packs (Cobra Earth Borer;		

Cobra Mountain Climber; Cobra Pom-Pom Gun;
Cobra Rope Crosser; G.I. Joe Helicopter;
G.I. Joe Rope Walker, G.I. Joe Anti-Aircraft Gun;

G.I. Joe Radar Station)	3-4 ea.	10-12 ea. MOC
Persuader (with Back-Stop)	12-15	35 (65+ MISB)
POGO	8-10	15 (30+ MISB)
Road-Toad B.R.V.	5-6	12 (20-25 MISB)
Sea Ray (with Sea Slug)	12-15	25 (50-55 MISB)
S.L.A.M.	6-8	12 (22-25 MISB)
Wolf (with Ice Viper)	22-26	35 (70-75+ MISB)

Battle Force 2000 vehicles

All of the following combine to make the BF 2000 Future Fortress, which
was never sold together; all vehicles sold separately.

Dominator	6-8	12-15 (20-25 MISB)
Eliminator	15-18	20-22 (28-30 MISB)
Marauder	6-8	12-15 (20-25 MISB)
Sky Sweeper	6-8	12-15 (20-25 MISB)
Vector	15-18	22-25 (35-40 MISB)
Vindicator	6-8	12-15 (20-25 MISB)

Series 7 (1988)

Figures, individually carded

Astro-Viper	10	25-30
Blizzard	12-15	25-30
Budo	12	25-30
Charbroil	15	25-30
Hardball	10-12	20-25
Hit & Run	12-15	25
Hydro Viper	10-12	25
Iron Grenadiers	13-16	25-30+
Lightfoot	12-15	20-25
Muskrat	10-12	25
Repeater	10-12	20-25

Road Pig	13-17	25-30
Shockwave	12-15	35-40+
Spearhead and Max	12-15	25-30
Storm Shadow	16-22	40-50
Toxo-Viper	8-10	25
Voltar	6-8	12-15

Night Force (Toys 'R Us exclusives, two-packs)

Night Force Crazylegs (with NF Outback)	25-30	80-100 MOC (two-pack)
Night Force Lt. Falcon (with NF Sneak Peek)	30-35	80-100 MOC (two-pack)
Night Force Outback	35-40	(see above)
Night Force Psyche-Out (with NF Tunnel Rat)	30-35	80-100 MOC (two-pack)
Night Force Sneak Peek	30-35	(see above)
Night Force Tunnel Rat	35-40	(see above)

Tiger Force

Bazooka	10-12	30-35
Duke	12-15	35-40
Dusty	10-12	35-40
Flint	10-12	30-35
Lifeline	8-10	25-30
Roadblock	12-15	32-38
Tripwire	8-10	35-40

Figures, vehicle drivers

Armadillo (Rolling Thunder Driver)	6-8	n/a
Destro (with the Despoiler)	10-12	n/a
Ferret (Iron Grenadier D.E.M.O.N. Drivers)	8-10	n/a
Ghostrider (Phantom X-19 Pilot)	12-15	n/a
Nullifier (Iron Grenadiers A.G.P. Pilot)	8-10	n/a
Sgt. Slaughter (Drill Instructor;		

Warthog A.I.F.V.)	10-12	n/a
Secto Viper (Cobra BUGG Driver)	15-20	n/a
Skidmark (Desert Fox Driver)	6-8	n/a
Star Viper (Cobra Stellar Stiletto Pilot)	6-8	n/a
Wild Card (Mean Dog Driver)	10-12	n/a
Windmill (Skystorm X-Wing Chopper Pilot)	6-8	n/a

Tiger Force

Frostbite (Tiger Cat Driver)	8-10	n/a
Recondo (Tiger Fly Pilot)	10-12	n/a
Skystriker (Tiger Rat Pilot)	22-25	n/a

Figures, mail-away and exclusives

Hit & Run, Target exclusive (with Parachute Pack)	25-30	350-400+ (MOC)
Super Trooper	6-8	15-18
		(mint in baggie)
Ultimate Enemies: Muskrat versus Voltar		
(two-pack; Target exclusive)	12-15	275+ (MOC)

Vehicles, Playsets, and Accessories

A.G.P. (with Nullifier)	10-12	18-25 (40-45+ MISB)
Battle Gear Accessory Pack #6	5	10-15 (MOC)
Cobra Adder	5	8-12 (15 MISB)
Cobra Battle Barge	5	8-12 (15 MISB)
Cobra BUGG (with Secto-Viper)	35-40	50-55 (110-125+ MISB)
Cobra Imp	5	8-12 (15 MISB)
Cobra Stellar Stiletto (with Star Viper)	10-12	15-20 (50+ MISB)
D.E.M.O.N. (with Ferret)	15-18	25-30 (70+ MISB)
Desert Fox 6-WD (with Skidmark)	10-12	18-25 (75+ MISB)
Destro's Despoiler (with Destro)	12	20-22 (45-50+ MISB)
Mean Dog (with Wild Card)	22-25	35 (100+ MISB)
Motorized Action Packs: Cobra Machine Gun Nest; Cobra Twin Missile Radar; Dreadnok Battle Ax; G.I. Joe Double Machine Gun; G.I. Joe Mine Sweeper; G.I. Joe Mortar Launcher	4-6 ea.	8-12 MOC ea.

Motorized Vehicle Packs: Cobra Gyrocopter;
Cobra Rocket Sled; G.I. Joe A.T.V.;
G.I. Joe Double Machine Gun; G.I. Joe Mortar Launcher;

G.I. Joe Tank Car	5-7 ea.	8-14 MOC ea.
Phantom X-19 (with Ghostrider)	40-45	65-75
		(150-160+ MISB)
Rolling Thunder (with Armadillo)	45-55	65 (110-125 MISB)
R.P.V. (Remote Piloted Vehicle)	5	10 (12-15 MISB)
Skystorm Cross-Wing Chopper (with Windmill)	12-15	32-35
		(65-75+ MISB)
Swampmasher	6-8	10-12 (20-25 MISB)
Warthog A.I.F.V. (with Sgt. Slaughter)	14-18	20-25
		(90-100 MISB)

Night Force vehicles

Night Blaster (NF Maggot)	40-45	75
		(160-175+ MISB)
Night Raider (NF Triple "T")	12-15	25 (65 MISB)
Night Shade (NF S.H.A.R.C.)	15-18	25-28 (75 MISB)
Night Storm (Persuader)	25-28	40
		(110-125+ MISB)
Night Striker (W.H.A.L.E.)	200-225+	300 (500+ MISB)

Tiger Force vehicles

Tiger Cat (TF Snow Cat)	22-28	35 (65+ MISB)
Tiger Fly (TF Dragonfly)	25-30	40 (90 MISB)
Tiger Paw (TF Ferret)	12-15	30 (45+ MISB)
Tiger Rat (TF Rattler)	32-38	60
		(175-200+ MISB)
Tiger Shark (TF Water Moccasin)	22-25	35 (60+ MISB)

Series 8 (1989)

Figures, individually carded

Alley Viper	20-22+	45-50
Annihilator	12-15	25

Backblast	12	20-25
Countdown	12	20-25
Dee-Jay	8-10	15-20
Deep Six	10-12	20-25
Downtown	10	15-20
Frag-Viper	14-18	28-35
Gnawgahyde	12-15	22-26
H.E.A.T. Viper	10-12	20-22
Night Viper	14-18	40-45
Recoil	10-12	15-20
Rock 'n Roll	12-15	20-22
Scoop	10-12	20-22
Snake Eyes	18-22	40-45+
Stalker	14-16	22-26
T.A.R.G.A.T.	10-12	20-25

Night Force (Toys 'R Us exclusives, two-packs)

Night Force Charbroil (with NF Repeater)	35-45	90-110+ MOC
Night Force Lightfoot (with NF Shockwave)	35-45	90-110+ MOC
Night Force Muskrat (with NF Spearhead and Max)	35-45	90-110+ MOC
Night Force Repeater	35-45	(see above)
Night Force Shockwave	40-45	(see above)
Night Force Spearhead and Max	35-45	(see above)

Python Patrol

Python Patrol Copperhead	10	22-25
Python Crimson Guard	10	22-25
Python Officer	12-15	32
Python Tele-Viper	10	22
Python Trooper	12-15	32
Python Viper	15	30-35

Slaughter's Marauders

Barbecue	10-12	18-25

Footloose	10-12	18-25
Low-Light	10-12	18-25
Mutt	12-15	20-25
Sgt. Slaughter	10-12	18-25
Spirit	10-12	18-25

Figures, mail-aways

Lifeline (Kellog's Rice Krispies)	4-6	10-12 (mint in baggie)
Rampage	6-8	16-20 (mint in baggie)

Figures, vehicle drivers

Aero-Viper (Cobra Condor Pilot)	12-14	n/a
Darklon (Evader Driver)	10	n/a
Dogfight (Mudfighter Pilot)	8	n/a
Hot Seat (Raider Driver)	10	n/a
Long Range (Thunderclap Driver)	8	n/a
Payload (Crusader Pilot)	22-26	n/a
Track Viper (Cobra H.I.S.S. Driver)	8	n/a
Wild Boar (Destro's Razorback Driver)	8	n/a
Windchill (Arctic Blast Driver)	8	n/a

Vehicles, Playsets, and Accessories

Arctic Blast (with Windchill)	12	20 (45-55+ MISB)
Battle Force 2000 Pulverizer	5	10 (15-20 MISB)
Battlefield Robot Radar Rat	4-5	8 (12 MISB)
Battlefield Robot Tri-Blaster	4-5	8 (12 MISB)
Cobra Battlefield Robot Devastator	4-5	8 (12 MISB)
Cobra Battlefield Robot Hovercraft	4-5	8 (12 MISB)
Cobra Condor Z-25 (with Aero-Viper)	50-55+	70 (160-170+ MISB)
Cobra FANG II	6	10 (25+ MISB)
Cobra H.I.S.S. II (with Track Viper)	10-12	25-30 (75-80+ MISB)
Crusader Space Shuttle (with Avenger Scout Craft and Payload [yellow highlights])	45-55	70 (115+ MISB)
Darklon's Evader (with Darklon)	10	15 (25-30+ MISB)
Destro's Razorback (with Wild Boar)	18-25	35 (65-70+ MISB)

Mudfighter (with Dogfight)	12	25 (55+ MISB)
Raider (with Hot Seat)	20-25	35 (65-75+ MISB)
Thunderclap (with Long Range)	35-45	60 (90-95+ MISB)

Night Force vehicles

Night Boomer (NF Skystriker)	250	350 (500+ MISB)
Night Scrambler (NF A.P.C.)	35-40	50-55 (100+ MISB)
Night Ray (NF Moray)	225-250	325 (485-500+ MISB)

Python Patrol vehicles

Python A.S.P.	12-15	20 (35 MISB)
Python Conquest	18-25	40-45 (65-70+ MISB)
Python STUN	20-22	35-40 (60-65+ MISB)

Slaughter's Marauders vehicles

Armadillo (SM modified Armadillo)	12-15	25 (35+ MISB)
Equalizer (SM modified Mauler)	35-45	60 (85-95+ MISB)
Lynx (SM modified Wolverine)	15-18	25 (50+ MISB)

Tiger Force

Tiger Fish (TF Devilfish)	15-18	25 (40-45+ MISB)
Tiger Sting (TF Vamp Mark II)	22-25	30 (60+ MISB)

Series 9 (1990)

Figures, individually carded

Ambush	8	10-15
Bullhorn	15-20	25-30
Captain Grid-Iron	6-8	10-12
Freefall	8	10-15
Laser-Viper	8	10-15
Metalhead	8	10-15
Night Creeper	12-15	22-25
Pathfinder	8	10-15
Rampart	8	10-15
Range-Viper	12-15	25-30
Rock Viper	10-12	15-18

G.I. Joe 3-3/4": Sub-Zero, Hasbro, 1990, $18 MIP.

Salvo	12-15	25-30
S.A.W. Viper	8-10	30-35
Stretcher	10-12	25
Sub-Zero	10-12	15-18
Topside	8	12-15
Undertow	10	20-22

Sonic Fighters

Dial-Tone	8-10	14-16
Dodger	8-10	14-16
Lampreys	8-10	20-25
Law	8-10	14-16
Tunnel Rat	8-10	14-16
Viper	12-15	25-30

Sky Patrol

Airborne	15-18	35-40
Airwave	15-18	35-40
Altitude	15-18	35-40
Drop Zone	15-18	35-40
Skydive	15-18	35-40
Static Line	15-18	35-40

Figures, exclusives
Rapid Fire (Toys 'R Us)

Figures, vehicle drivers

Cold Front (Avalanche Driver, with microphone) 25-30+		n/a
Cold Front (without microphone)	10-12	n/a
Decimator (Cobra Hammerhead Driver)	14-18	n/a
Major Storm (General Driver)	15-20	n/a
Overlord (Cobra Dictator)	8-10	n/a
Updraft (Retaliator Pilot)	15-20+	n/a
Vapor (Cobra Hurricane Pilot)	12-15	n/a

Vehicles, Playsets, and Accessories

Avalanche (with Cold Front)	20-25	35-45 (85-95+ MISB)
Cobra Hammerhead (with Hammerhead)	45-55	80-90 (200-210+ MISB)
Cobra Piranha	10-12	15 (25 MISB)
Cobra Rage	20-25	40 (85-90+ MISB)
Destro's Dominator	20-22	30-32 (60-65+ MISB)
G.I. Joe General (with Major Storm)	75+	110-120 (290+ MISB)
Locust from G.I. Joe General	35-45+	n/a
Hammer	35-40	65-70 (100+ MISB)
Hurricane V.T.O.L. (with Vapor)	40-45	55-60 (160-175+ MISB)
Locust	10-12	18 (25+ MISB)
Mobile Battle Bunker	10-12	20 (35+ MISB)
Overlord's Dictator (with Overlord)	5-6	12 (25-30+ MISB)
Retaliator (with Updraft)	35-45	55 (125-135+ MISB)

Sky Patrol vehicles

Sky Havoc	20-22	30-35 (50-60 MISB)
Sky Hawk	12	18-20 (30-35+ MISB)
Sky Raven	75-80	110-120 (175+ MISB)
Sky SHARC	10-12	22 (35-40 MISB)

Series 10 (1991)

Figures, individually carded

Big Ben	10	15-20
Cobra B.A.T.	10	15-20
Cobra Commander	12-15	20-22
Crimson Guard Immortal	15	25-30
Desert Scorpion	12-15	25
Dusty and Sandstorm	10	15-20
General Hawk	10	15-20
Grunt	10	15-20
Heavy Duty	10	15-20
Incinerators	12-15	20-22
Low-Light	10	15-20
Mercer	10	15-20

Red Star (G.I. Joe cardback)	10	15-20
Red Star (Cobra cardback)	10	55-75+
Sci-Fi	10	15-20
Snake-Eyes	14	22-28
Snow Serpent	10	15-20
Tracker	10	15-20

Figures, vehicle drivers

Cloudburst (with glider)	8-10	n/a
Interrogator (with Battle Copter)	8-10	n/a
Major Altitude (with Battle Copter)	8	n/a
Night Vulture (with glider)	10-12	n/a
Sky Creeper (with glider)	8-10	n/a
Skymate (with glider)	15-18	n/a

Eco-Warriors

Cesspool	6	12
Cobra Toxo-Viper	10-12	15-18
Clean Sweep	6	12
Flint	6	12
Ozone	6	12
Sludge Viper	10-12	15-18

Super Sonic Fighters

Lt. Falcon	6-8	12-15
Major Bludd	8-10	15
Psyche-Out	10-12	15-20
Road Pig	8-10	15
Rock 'n Roll	8-10	15
Zap	10-12	15-20

Talking Battle Commanders

Cobra Commander	4-6	10-12
Hawk	4-6	10-12
Overkill	4-6	10-12
Stalker	4-6	10-12

Vehicles, Playsets, and Accessories

Attack Cruiser	6	10-12 (15-20 MISB)
Badger	8-10	12-15 (25 MISB)
Battle Wagon	15-18	20-25 (30+ MISB)
Brawler	10-12	12-15 (25+ MISB)
Cobra Battle Copter (with Interrogator)	5	12-15 (20+ MISB)
Cobra Air Commando Glider (with Night Vulture)	10-12	30-35+ (MOC)
Cobra Air Commando Glider (with Sky Creeper)	10-12	30-35+ (MOC)
Cobra Ice Saber	8-10	15 (25 MISB)
Cobra Paralyzer	8-10	15 (25 MISB)
Cobra Septic Tank	8-10	15 (25 MISB)
G.I. Joe Battle Copter (with Major Altitude)	5	12-15 (20+ MISB)
G.I. Joe Air Commando Glider (with Cloudburst)	10-12	30-35+ (MOC)
G.I. Joe Air Commando Glider (with Skymate)	10-12	35-40+ (MOC)

Series 11 (1992)

Figures, individually carded

Battle Corps

Barricade (Battle Corps #9)	4-6	10-12
Big Bear (BC #4)	4-6	10-12
Cobra Eel (BC #12)	4-6	10-12
Destro (BC #5)	4-6	12-15
Duke (BC #1)	4-6	10-12
Firefly (BC #11)	4-6	10-12
Flak Viper (BC #6)	4-6	10-12
General Flagg (BC #7)	4-6	10-12
Gung-Ho (BC #8)	4-6	10-12

Roadblock (recalled version, with rare launcher BC #3)	65-75+	175-200+
Wet Suit (BC #2)	4-6	10-12
Wild Bill (BC #10)	4-6	10-12

D.E.F.

Bullet Proof (D.E.F. #1)	4-6	10-12
Cutter (D.E.F. #5)	4-6	10-12
Evil Headhunter (D.E.F. #6)	4-6	10-12
Headman (D.E.F. #4)	4-6	10-12
Mutt and Junkyard (D.E.F. #3)	6-8	12-15
Shockwave (D.E.F. #2)	10-12	20-22

Eco-Warriors

Barbecue (Eco-Warriors)	4-6	10-12
Deep-Six (Eco-Warriors)	4-6	10-12
Toxo-Zombie (Eco-Warriors)	4-6	10-12

Ninja Force

Dice (Ninja Force I #6)	4-6	10-12
Dojo (Ninja Force I #2)	4-6	10-12
Nunchuck (Ninja Force I #3)	4-6	10-12
Slice (Ninja Force - red I #5)	4-6	10-12
Storm Shadow (Ninja Force I #1)	6	12
T'jbang (Ninja Force I #4)	4-6	10-12

Figures, mail-aways

Ninja Viper (no swords)	15-18	(25+ mint in baggie)
Ninja Viper (two swords)	40-45	(50-60 mint in baggie)

Figures, vehicle drivers

Ace (Battle Copter Pilot)	6-8	n/a
Cobra Air Devil (Acrobatic Aerial Assault Trooper)	12-15	n/a
Heli-Viper (Cobra Battle Coptor Pilot)	6-8	n/a
Spirit (Air Commandos Leader)	10-12	n/a

G.I. Joe 3-3/4": Deep Six, Hasbro, 1992, $12 MIP.

Vehicles, Playsets, and Accessories

Advanced Tactical Fighter: Liquidator	8	15 (25 MISB)
Advanced Tactical Fighter: Storm Eagle	8	15 (25 MISB)
AH-74 Desert Apache	25-30	45-50 (85-95+ MISB)
Barracuda	5	10-12 (20+ MISB)
Cobra Battle Copter (Heli-Viper's)	5	10-12 (20+ MISB)
Cobra Earthquake	8-12	15 (25-30+ MISB)
Cobra Air Commandos Glider (Air Devil's)	8-12	30+ (MOC)
Cobra Parasite	8-10	15 (25+ MISB)
Cobra Rat	6	10-12 (20+ MISB)
Cobra Toxo-Lab Playset	30+	35-40 (75+ MISB)
Eco-Striker	10	12-15 (30+ MISB)
Fort America	12-15	20 (35+ MISB)
G.I. Joe Battle Copter (Ace's)	5	10-12 (20+ MISB)
G.I. Joe Air Commandos Glider (Spirit's)	10-12	30-35+ (MOC)
G.I. Joe Headquarters	35-40	45+ (80-90+MISB)
Patriot	10-12	20-22 (30+ MISB)

Series 12 (1993)

Note: The "BC" numbers below indicate the Battle Corps series numbers that Hasbro assigned to display the figures on the package backs.

Figures, individually carded

Alley Viper (Battle Corps #6)	8	10-12
Backblast (BC #22)	4-6	10-12
Barricade (BC #17)	4-6	10-12
Bazooka (BC #1)	4-6	10-12
Beach-Head (BC #4)	4-6	10-12
Bullet-Proof (BC #34)	4-6	10-12
Cobra Commander (BC #24)	6	10-12
Cobra Eel (BC #27)	6	10-12
Colonel Courage (BC #10)	4-6	10-12
Crimson Guard Commander (BC#23)	6-8	12-15
Cross-Country (BC #2)	4-6	10-12

Dr. Mindbender (BC #15)	4-6	10-12
Duke (BC #19)	4-6	10-12
Firefly (BC #18)	4-6	10-12
Flak-Viper (BC #9)	4-6	10-12
Frostbite (BC #20)	4-6	10-12
General Flagg (BC #26)	4-6	10-12
Gristle (BC #32)	4-6	10-12
Gung-Ho (BC #16)	4-6	10-12
Headhunters (BC #35)	4-6	10-12
Headhunter Stormtroopers (BC #33)	15-18	25+
H.E.A.T. Viper (BC #5)	4-6	10-12
Iceberg (BC #3)	4-6	10-12
Keel-Haul (BC #21)	4-6	10-12
Law (BC #28)	4-6	10-12
Leatherneck (BC #11)	4-6	10-12
Long Arm (BC #31)	4-6	10-12
Mace (BC #29)	4-6	10-12
Muskrat (BC #30)	4-6	10-12
Mutt and Junkyard (BC #36)	4-6	10-12
Night Creeper Leader (BC #14)	4-6	10-12
Outback (BC #13)	4-6	10-12
Roadblock (BC #7)	4-6	10-12
Snowstorm (BC #12)	4-6	10-12
Wet-Suit (BC #8)	4-6	10-12
Wild Bill (BC #25)	4-6	10-12

Mega-Marines

Bio-Vipers	4-6	10
Blast-Off	4-6	10
Clutch	4-6	10-12
Cyber Vipers	4-6	12-15
Gung-Ho	4-6	10-12
Mega Vipers	4-6	12-15
Mirage	4-6	10
Monstro-Vipers	4-6	10

Ninja Force

Banzai (Ninja Force II, #5)	4-6	10
Bushido (Ninja Force II, #6)	4-6	10
Night Creeper (Ninja Force II, #3)	4-6	10
Scarlett (Ninja Force II, #4)	4-6	10-12
Slice (Ninja Force II- orange #7)	4-6	10
Snake Eyes (Ninja Force II, #1)	4-6	10-12
Zartan (Ninja Force II, #2)	4-6	10-12

Ninja Force vehicle drivers

Red Ninjas (Battle Axe Driver)	6-8	12+
T'Gin-Zu (Pile Driver Operator)	6-8	10-12

Star Brigade

Astro-Viper (#11)	4-6	10
Countdown (#8)	4-6	10
Ozone (#10)	6	10-12
Payload (#7)	4-6	10
Roadblock (#9)	4-6	10
T.A.R.G.A.T. (#12)	4-6	10

Star Brigade vehicle drivers

Sci-Fi (Star Brigade Starfighter Pilot)

Star Brigade Armor-Tech

Cobra B.A.A.T. (#6)	4-6	10
Destro (#5)	4-6	10
Duke (#2)	4-6	10
Heavy Duty (#4)	4-6	10
Robo-Joe (#1)	4-6	10
Rock 'n Roll (#3)	4-6	10

Street Fighter II Figures, individually carded

Balrog (#11)	6-8	15-20
Blanka (#5)	6	12

Chun-Li (#4)	6	12
Dhalsim (#8)	6	12
Edmond Honda (#7)	6	12
Guile (#3)	6	12
Ken Masters (#2)	6	12
M. Bison (#6)	6	12
Ryu (#1)	6	12
Sagat (#12)	6-8	15-20
Vega (#10)	6-8	15-20
Zangief (#9)	6-8	15-20

Street Fighter II Vehicle drivers

Blanka (with Beast Blaster)	6-8	n/a
Chun-Li (with Beast Blaster)	6-8	n/a
Guile (Sonic Boom Tank Driver)	6	n/a
Ken Masters (with Dragon Fortress)	8	n/a
M. Bison (Crimson Cruiser Driver)	6	n/a
Ryu (with Dragon Fortress)	8	n/a

Figures, mail-away

Create-A-Cobra (no filecard) labels)	15-20	(35+ mint in baggie with
Create-A-Cobra (with filecard)	45-50	(60+ mint in baggie [inside a mailer box])
Deep Six (fluorescent)	6-8	(12-15 mint in baggie)
Hawk ("Sonic," bright colors)	6	(10 mint in baggie)

Arctic Commandos

(four-pack)	18-22	(35-40 MISP)
Dee-Jay	6-8	n/a
Snow-Serpent	6-8	n/a
Stalker	6-8	n/a
Sub-Zero	6-8	n/a

Battle Copter Pilots

(two-pack)	12-15	(20-22+ MISP)

Interrogator	6-8	n/a
Major Altitude	6-8	n/a

International Action Force
(four-pack)	20-25	(40-45 MISP)
Big Bear	8-10	n/a
Big Ben	8-10	n/a
Budo	8-10	n/a
Spirit	8-10	n/a

Rapid Deployment Force
(three-pack with black-colored pocket patrol pack; no accessories)	15-18	(35-40+ MISP)
Fast Draw	4-6	n/a
Night Force Repeater	8-10	n/a
Night Force Shockwave	8-10	n/a

Figures, vehicle drivers
Ace (Fighter Pilot)	8-10	n/a
Ambush (Dino Hunters Playset)	20-25	n/a
Cutter (Coast Guard Specialist)	6-8	n/a
Low-Light (Dino Hunters Playset)	20-25	n/a
Nitro-Viper (Detonator Driver)	10-12	n/a

Vehicles, Playsets, and Accessories
Armor-Bot (with General Hawk)	12-18	20-25 (35-45+ MISB)
Cobra Detonator (with Nitro-Viper)	10-12	15-18 (35-40 MISB)
Cobra Invader	6-8	10 (15-18 MISB)
Dino Hunter Mission Playset (with Ambush and Low-Light)	25-30	40+ (60-70+ MISB)
Ghoststriker X-16 (with Ace)	18-25	35-40 (65+ MISB)
Ice Snake	6-8	12 (20 MISB)
Mudbuster	6-8	12 (20 MISB)
SHARK 9000 (with Cutter)	6-8	12 (20 MISB)

Mega-Marines Vehicles
Monster Blaster A.P.C.	10-12	25-30 (45 MISB)

G.I. Joe 3-3/4": Ice Cream Soldier, Hasbro, 1994, $10 MIP.

Ninja Force Vehicles

Ninja Lightning	5	8 (12-15 MISB)
Ninja Raider Battle Ax (with Red Ninjas)	6-8	12 (30 MISB)
Ninja Raider Pile Driver (with T-Gin-Zu)	6-8	12 (30 MISB)

Star Brigade Vehicles

Starfighter (with Sci-Fi)	10-12	15-20 (25-30 MISB)

Street Fighter Vehicles

Beast Blaster (with Chun-Li and Blanka)	15-22	25-28 (35+ MISB)
Crimson Cruiser (with M. Bison)	6-8	10-12 (20-25 MISB)
Dragon Fortress (with Ken Masters and Ryu)	18-25	35-40 (50-60+ MISB)

Series 13 (1994)

Figures, individually carded

Battle Corps

Alley-Viper (BC #7)	8-10	12-15
Beach-Head (BC #6)	6-8	10-12
Dial-Tone (BC #2)	6-8	12
Flint (BC #1)	6-8	12
Ice Cream Soldier (BC #10)	4-6	10
Lifeline (BC #8)	6-8	12-15
Major Bludd (BC #11)	6-8	12
Metal-Head (BC #4)	6-8	12
Night Creeper-Leader (BC #13)	6-8	12-15
Shipwreck (BC #3)	6-8	12
Snowstorm (BC #12)	4-6	10
Stalker (BC #9)	4-6	10
(Infantry) Viper (BC, #5)	6-8	12

Shadow Ninjas

Bushido (#39)	4-6	10
Night Creeper (#42)	4-6	10

G.I. Joe 3-3/4": Battle Corps Lifeline, Hasbro, 1994, $15 MIP.

G.I. Joe 3-3/4": Battle Corps Major Bludd, Hasbro, 1994, $12 MIP.

G.I. Joe 3-3/4": Battle Corps Night Creeper Leader, Hasbro, 1994, $15 MIP.

G.I. Joe 3-3/4": Battle Corps Snow Storm, Hasbro, 1994, $10 MIP.

G.I. Joe 3-3/4": Battle Corps Stalker, Hasbro, 1994, $10 MIP.

Nunchuk (#41)	4-6	10
Slice (#40)	4-6	10
Snake Eyes (#37)	4-6	10-12
Storm Shadow (#38)	4-6	10-12

Star Brigade

Carcass (#52)	4-6	12-15
Cobra Blackstar (#25)	8-10	15-18
Cobra Commander (#24)	8-10	15-20+
Countdown (#53)	4-6	12
Duke (#21)	6-8	12-15
Effects (#49)	6-8	12-15
Lobotomaxx (#50)	6-8	12-15
Ozone (#54)	6-8	12
Payload (#26)	6-8	12
Predacon (#51)	10-12	15-20
Roadblock (#27)	6-8	12
Sci-Fi (#22)	6-8	12-14
Space Shot (#23)	8-10	12-15

Figures, mail-aways

G.I. Joe (Joseph Colton Mail-Away)	4-6	10-12 (mint in baggie)

Figures, vehicle drivers

Gears (Star Brigade, Invention Technician, #60)	6-8	n/a
Techno-Viper (Star Brigade, Cobra Battlefield Technician, #61)	12-15	n/a
Windchill (Blockbuster Driver, #62)	6-8	n/a

30th Anniversary

Boxed Set (and individually boxed)	15-18	(25-30+ MISP)
Action Marine (30th Anniversary boxed set)	6-8	n/a
Action Marine (sold separately, boxed)	4-6	8-10 MIB
Action Pilot (30th Anniversary boxed set)	6-8	n/a
Action Pilot (sold separately, boxed)	4-6	8-10 MIB

Action Pilot Astronaut		
(30th Anniversary boxed set)	6-8	n/a
Action Pilot Astronaut (sold separately, boxed)	4-6	8-10 MIB
Action Sailor (30th Anniversary boxed set)	6-8	n/a
Action Sailor (sold separately, boxed)	4-6	8-10 MIB
Action Soldier (30th Anniversary boxed set)	6-8	n/a
Action Soldier (sold separately, boxed)	4-6	8-10 MIB

Vehicles, Playsets, and Accessories

Action Pilot, Action Astronaut Space Capsule		
(Original Action Team)	6-8	n/a
Blockbuster	15-20	25 (45+ MISB)
Manta Ray	4-6	10 (15-20 MISB)
Razor-Blade	15-20	25 (30-35 MISB)
Scorpion	6-8	12-15 (25 MISB)

Star Brigade Vehicles

Power-Fighter (Cobra)	30-35	50-55
Power-Fighter (G.I. Joe)	18-25	40-45

Series 14 (1997)
All are Toys 'R Us exclusives.

Figures

Cobra Command Team

(carded set)	15-18	(25-28+ MOC)
Baroness	6-8	n/a
Cobra Commander	6-8	n/a
Destro	6-8	n/a

G.I. Joe Arctic Mission

(carded set)	12-15	(18-22 MOC)
Blizzard	4-6	n/a
Iceberg	4-6	n/a
Snow Job	4-6	n/a

G.I. Joe Commando Team

(carded set)	18-22	(28-35+ MOC)
Lady Jaye	8-10	n/a
Snake Eyes	8-10+	n/a
Storm Shadow	8-10+	n/a

Mission Packs

Army Recon Mission

(carded set)	10-12	(15-20 MOC)
Duke	4-6	n/a
Silver Mirage Motorcycle (vehicle)	4-6	n/a

Cobra Viper Team

(carded set)	25-28	35-40+
Cobra Infantry Trooper	15	n/a
Cobra Flight Pod (vehicle)	10-12	n/a

Navy S.E.A.L. Mission

(carded set)	8-10	(15-28 MOC)
Night Landing (vehicle)	4-6	n/a
Torpedo	4-6	n/a

Stars and Stripes Forever

(figure set)	28-32	(45-50+ MISP)
Breaker	5	n/a
Grunt	5	n/a
Rock and Roll	5-6	n/a
Scarlett	6-8	n/a
Sgt. Zap	5	n/a
Short Fuze	5	n/a
Snake Eyes	8-10	n/a
Stalker	5-6	n/a

Vehicles, Playsets, and Accessories

A-10 Thunderbolt (with General Hawk [$6-8] and Ace [$15-20])	40-45	50-55 (75-80+ MISB)

Cobra Rage (with Alley Viper [$8-10])	18-20	25 (35-40+ MISB)
Slugger (with Gung-Ho [$4-6])	8-10	15 (25-30 MISB)

Series 15 (1998)

All are Toys 'R Us exclusives.

Figures

Cobra Infantry Team

(carded set)	35-40	(65-70+ MOC)
Cobra Officer	12-15+	n/a
Cobra Trooper (x2)	12-15+ ea.	n/a

Cobra Polar Force

(carded set)	25-30	(38-40+ MOC)
Firefly	12-15+	n/a
Night Creeper	8-10	n/a
Snow Serpent	8-10	n/a

G.I. Joe Navy Assault Unit

(carded set)	15-18	(22-25+ MOC)
Shipwreck	5-6	n/a
Torpedo	5-6	n/a
Wet-Suit	5-6	n/a
Oktober Guard		
(carded set)	12-15	(18-25+ MOC)
Colonel Brekhov	6-8	n/a
Lieutenant Gorky	6-8	n/a
Volga	6-8	n/a

Vehicles, Playsets, and Accessories

Conquest X-30 (with Ace [$12-15])	22-25	30-35 (45-50+ MISB)
MOBAT (with Heavy Duty [$6-8] and Thunderwing [$6-8])	22-25	28-30 (35+ MISB)
Rattler 4WD (with Vypra [$20-25])	30-35	38-42 (60-65+ MISB)

(He-Man and the...) Masters of the Universe
(Mattel, 1982-87)

Series 1 (1982)

Figures, individually carded

Beast Man	15-20	180+
He-Man	18-20	250+
Man-At-Arms	10-12	180+
Mer-Man	12-15	170+
Skeletor	18-20	240+
Stratos	10-12	180+
Teela	18-20	215+
Zodac	10-12	150+

Mail-order

He-Man (Wonder Bread)	225+	500+ MISP

Vehicles, Playsets, and Accessories

Battle Cat	15	50
Battle Ram	10-12	20-25
Castle Grayskull playset	60-80+	100-110
		(with all accessories)
		(250+ MISB)
Wind Raider	10-12	20-25

Series 2 (1983)

Figures, individually carded; reissues from Series 1

Beast Man	15-20	70-75+
He-Man	18-20	120+
Man-At-Arms	10-12	60+
Mer-Man	12-15	60+
Skeletor	18-20	110+
Stratos	10-12	60+
Teela	18-20	90+
Zodac	10-12	60+

He-Man and the Masters of the Universe Wind Raider, Series 1, Mattel, 1982, $25 MIP.

He-Man and the Masters of the Universe Panthor, Series 2, Mattel, 1983, $45 MIP.

Figures, individually carded; new figures

Evil-Lyn	20-25	135+
Faker	25-35	280+
Man-E-Faces	8-10	65+
Man-E-Faces (with extra weapons set)	75-85	550+
Mekaneck	8	60+
Ram Man	12	60+
Trap Jaw	13-16	65-70+
Tri-Klops	10-12	60+

Vehicles, Playsets, and Accessories

Attak Trak	10-12	25
Panthor	15	45
Point Dead and Talon Fighter	20	75
Road Ripper	10	25
Screech	15	35-40
Zoar	15	30

Series 3 (1984)

Figures, individually carded

Battle Armor He-Man	15-20	60+
Battle Armor Skeletor	10-14	45+
Buzz-Off	10-12	40
Clawful	10-12	40
Fisto	10-12	40
Jitsu	10-12	40
Kobra Khan	12-15	55
Prince Adam	15-20	60-65
Orko	15-20	45-50
Webstor	12-15	40
Whiplash	10	35

Vehicles, Playsets, and Accessories

Dragon Walker	12-15	40-45

He-Man and the Masters of the Universe Dragon Walker, Series 3, Mattel, 1984, $45 MIP.

He-Man and the Masters of the Universe Grizzlor, Series 4, Mattel, 1985, $40 MIP.

Roton	10	25
Snake Mountain Playset	65-75	110-125
		(200+ MISB)
Stridor	8	25-30
Weapons Pak	5	10

Series 4 (1985)

Figures, individually carded

Dragon Blaster Skeletor	15	35-40
Grizzlor	10-12	40
Hordak	15-20	65-70+
Leech	10-12	40
Mantenna	10-12	40
Modulok	12-15	35-40
Moss Man	8-10	40
Roboto	12-15	40
Rokkon	10-12	35
Spikor	10-12	40
Stinkor	8-10	40
Stonedar	10-12	35
Sy-Klone	10-12	40
Thunder-Punch He-Man	12-15	40
Two-Bad	8-10	40

Vehicles, Playsets, and Accessories

Bashasaurus	25	50
Battle Bones	10	20
Fright Zone playset	45-50	90-95
		(130-150+)
Land Shark	10-12	25
Night Stalker	10-12	25-30
Spydor	18-20	40-45

He-Man and the Masters of the Universe Slime Pit, Series 5, Mattel, 1986, $50 MIP.

Series 5 (1986)

Figures, individually carded

Dragstor	15-20	65-70+
Extendar	15-20	45-50
Flying Fists He-Man	15-20	45-50+
Horde Trooper	40	145-150+
Hurricane Hordak	15-20	60-65+
King Hiss	12-15	40-45+
Multi-Bot	15-20	40
Rattlor	12-15	40
Rio Blast	14-18	45-55+
Snout Spout	10-12	60-65
Terror Claws Skeletor	20-25	50-55
Tung Lashor	13-16	50-55

He-Man: The Masters of the Universe Movie figures

Blade	32-36	55-65
Gwildor	10-12	35-40
Saurod	22-28	35-42

Vehicles, Playsets, and Accessories

Beam Blaster and Artilleray	25-30	60
Blaster Hawk	25	60
Eternia playset	400+	650-700
		(900+ MISB)
Fright Fighter	12-15	45
Jet Sled	5	20
Laser Bolt	15	40
Matisaur	15	25-30
Megalaser	5	15
Monstroid (The Evil Horde)	15	50
Slime Pit	12-15	50
Slime Vat(s)	2	6
Stilt Stalkers	5	15-18

Meteorbs
Astro Lion, Comet Cat, Cometroid, Crocobite, Dinosorb, Gore-illa, Orebear,
    Rhinorb, Tuskor, Ty-Grrr   5-6 ea. loose   12-15 ea. MOC

Series 6 (1987)

Figures, individually carded

Blast-Attack	15-20	55+
Buzz-Saw Hordak	15-20	40-45
Clamp Champ	25-30	70-75
Faker (re-release)	12-15	75-100+
King Randor	40-45+	90+
Mosquitor	15-22	70-75
Ninjor	25-30	85-90+
Rotar	20-25	75-80+
Scare Glow	45-50	135-150+
Snake Face	15-22+	70-75
Sorceress	42-48	110-120+
Sssqueeze	15	70-75
Twistoid	45-50	80+

Vehicles, Playsets, and Accessories

Bionatops	25-30	45-50
Turbodactyl	25-30	60-65
Tyrantisaurus Rex	70-75	135-150

Foreign Releases (extremely rare)

Cliff Climber	20-25	50-60
Laser He-Man	150-175+	325+
Laser Skeletor	125-150+	310+
Megator (Italy only)	400	1350
Scubaattack	20-25	50-60
Tower Tools	20-25	50-60
Tytus (Italy only)	500	1450

Gift Sets (extremely rare)

Note: All gift sets should be considered extremely rare and prices should reflect this, but prices are in a constant state of flux. For figures packaged with an animal (i.e. He-Man and Battle Cat or Fisto and Stridor), prices come in at around $150-200 MIB or quite a bit more for mint and sealed samples ($250-300+). For triple-figure packs, I have seen prices over $400 for MISB samples. Again, these are quite rare, and it is up to the buyer and seller (and the current market) to decide what sale price is appropriate.

Battle Armor He-Man and Battle Cat (list continued on p. 203)

He-Man and the Masters of the Universe Rotar, Series 6, Mattel, 1987, $80 MIP.

He-Man and the Masters of the Universe, Reissue figures of Stratos, Clawful, and Buzz-Off, Mattel, 2000-01, $15 MIP each.

Battle Armor Skeletor and Land Shark
Battle for Eternia (Skeletor, Panthor, and Man-E-Faces)
Evil Horde (Hordak, Leech, and Mantenna)
Evil Warriors (Battle-Armor Skeletor, Webstor, and Mer-Man)
He-Man and Battle Cat
Fisto and Stridor
Flying Fists He-Man and Terror Claws Skeletor
Heroic Warriors (He-Man, Teela, and Ram-Man)
Jitsu and Nightstalker
Skeletor and Screech
Skeletor and Panthor

(He-Man and the…) Masters of the Universe, Reissues
(Mattel, 2000-01)

Figures, individually packaged

Battle Armor He-Man	5	15
Battle Armor Skeletor	5	15
Beast Man	5	15
Buzz-Off	5	15
Clawful	5	15
Evil-Lyn	5	15
Faker	5	20-25
He-Man	8-10	20
Man-At-Arms	5	15
Mer-Man	5	15
Skeletor	8-10	20
Stratos	5	15
Teela	5	15
Trap Jaw	5	15
Tri-Klops	5	15
Zodac	5	15

The Adventures of Indiana Jones: Indiana Jones figure, Series 1, Kenner, 1982, $300 MOMC.

Gift Sets

Figure 5-pack (with exclusive Moss Man)	25-28	45+
Figure 5-pack (with exclusive Prince Adam)	25-28	45+
Figure 10-pack (JC Penney's exclusive)	65-70	145+
He-Man and Battle Cat	20	45+
Skeletor with Panthor	20	45+

Indiana Jones, The Adventures of

(Kenner, 1982-83)

Note: These figures, vehicles, and playsets were based on the film, *Raiders of the Lost Ark*.

Series 1 (1982)

Figures

Indiana Jones	100+	250+ (300+ MOMC)
Marion Ravenwood	95-100+	300+ (300+ MOMC)
Toht	15	20+ (35+ MOMC)
Cairo Swordsman	15	20+ (35+ MOMC)
Belloq (mail-away)	10+20+	(20-25 mint in mailer box)

Playsets

Map Room	35-40	60 (110+ MISB)
Well of the Souls	55-60	85-90+ (190+ MISB)

Series 2 (1983)

Figures

Sallah	32-38	50+ (65+ MOMC)
Indiana Jones in German Uniform	20-25	50 (75+ MOMC)
German Mechanic	20-25	35 (45+ MOMC)

Belloq (MOC, only as a production sample, on second series card, same as the 1982 mail-away version, but carded. Extremely rare, 1 of only 3 surviving samples)
1000-1,000+

The Adventures of Indiana Jones: Well of the Souls playset, Series 1, Kenner, 1982, $190 MIB.

The Adventures of Indiana Jones: 12" Indiana Jones figure, Kenner, 1983, $250 MIB.

JLA (Justice League of America) Gift Set Collection III, Diamond Exclusive, Kenner, 2000, $30 MIP.

Vehicles, Playsets, and Accessories

Arabian Horse	50+	90+ (120+ MISB)
Streets of Cairo	45+	70 (100+ MISB)
Desert Convoy Truck	75+	100+ (140-150+ MISB)

12" figures

Indiana Jones	100	150+ (250+ MISB)

JLA (Justice League of America)
(Kenner, 1999-2000)

4" figures, individually carded

Series 1 (1999)

Batman	4	10-12
Flash (Wally West)	4	8
Green Arrow (Connor Hawk)	4	12-14
Green Lantern (Kyle Rayner)	4	8
Huntress	4	8
Superman Blue	3	5-7
Superman Red	3	5-7

Series 2 (1999)

Aquaman	3	5-7
Batman: The Dark Knight	10-12	25-30
(Classic) Superman	4	8
Martian Manhunter	3	5-7
Steel	3	5-7

Series 3 (2000)

Caped Crusader Batman	3	5-7
Impulse	4	8
Plastic Man	3	5-7
Robin	3	5-7
Superboy	3	5-7
Zauriel	4	8

Marvel Legends, Dr. Doom, Series 1, Toy Biz, 2002, $22 MIP.

Series 4 (Oct. 2000)

Atom, The	5-6	10-12
Batman	10	15-18
Red Tornado	5-6	12-15
Superman	5-6	12-15
Wonder Woman	10	15-18
Gift sets: Diamond exclusives		
Collection I (Green Lantern, Hologram Batman, Hologram Flash, Huntress, Superman Blue)	12-15	25-30
Collection II (Batman, Flash, Green Arrow, Hologram Green Lantern, Hologram Superman)	12-15	25-30
Collection III (Lex Luthor, Joker, Martian Manhunter, Superman, Zauriel)	12-15	25-30

10" figures

Martian Manhunter	4-6	10-12
Superman Blue	4-6	10-12

12" figures

Aquaman	6-8	14-16
Flash	6-8	14-16
Green Lantern	6-8	14-16

Marvel Legends
(Toy Biz 2002-present)

Note: Because of the nature of their articulation (most have 30+ points of articulation) and excellent sculpting, these figures are some of the hottest ever on the secondary market.

Series 1

Captain America	6-8	12-15
Hulk (articulated hands)	6-8	12-15
Hulk (non-bendable hands)	10-12	20-22
Iron Man	6-8	12-15
Iron Man with Gold Armor (variant)	30	55-60

Marvel Legends, The Punisher, Series 4, Toy Biz, 2002, $10 MIP.

Stealth Armor Iron Man (Wal-Mart exclusive)	50-55	75-85
Toad	22-28	55-65+

Series 2

Doombot (variant)	8-10	25-30
Dr. Doom	6-8	18-22
Hulk (with White Lab Coat)	6	12-15
Human Torch (with "4" symbol)	4-6	12-15
Human Torch (without "4" symbol)	4-6	10-12
Namor	4-6	12-15
The Thing	4-6	10-12
The Thing with Trenchcoat (Wal-Mart exclusive)	8-10	19-23

Series 3

Daredevil (bearded)	4-5	10
Daredevil (clean shaven)	4-5	10
Ghost Rider	6-8	15-18
Magneto	10-12	22-28
Thor	20-22	35-40
Wolverine	4-5	8-10
Wolverine Unmasked (variant)	15-20	75-80

Series 4

Beast	4-5	10
Elektra	4-5	10
Gambit	4-5	10-12
Goliath (variant)	10-12	30-35
Punisher (with Black Belt)	4-5	8-10
Punisher (with White Belt)	4-5	8-10

Series 5

Blade	8	16-20
Colossus	15-18	30-35
Mr. Fantastic	4-5	10
Nick Fury	4	8-10
Red Skull	12-15	40-45+

Marvel Legends, Red Skull, Series 5, Toy Biz, $45 MIP.

Marvel Famous Covers, Dark Phoenix, Toy Biz, $20 MIP.

Marvel Legends, Juggernaut, Series 6, Toy Biz, $35 MIP.

Marvel Famous Covers, Hawkeye, Toy Biz, $20 MIP.

Marvel Legends, Iceman, Series 8, Toy Biz, $15 MIP.

Sabretooth	8-10	18-22
Silver Surfer	4-5	8-10
Silver Surfer (variant; no Howard the Duck)	4-5	30-35

Series 6

Cable (brown highlights; variant)	12-15	35-40
Cable (yellow highlights)	6-8	10-12
Brown Wolverine	12	17-20
Dark Phoenix (variant)	20-25	65-70
Deadpool	8-10	20
Juggernaut	15-20	30-35
Phoenix	8-10	20
Punisher (Movie version)	4-5	10

Series 7

Apocalypse	12-15	25-30
Ghost Rider	5-6	10-12
Ghost Rider (phasing; variant)	15-18	35-40
Goliath	8-10	25-32
Hawkeye	8-10	15-20
Silver Centurion Iron Man	4-5	10-12
Vision	6-8	10-12
Vision (phasing; variant)	10-12	20-25
Weapon X	4-5	10

Series 8

Black Widow (blond hair; variant)	12-14	25-30
Black Widow (red hair)	8-10	15-22
Classic Captain America (variant)	8-10	22-25
Doc Ock	4-5	10-12
Iceman	6-8	15
Man-Thing	10-12	20-22
Modern Iron Man	6	12-14
Storm (with mohawk; variant)	12-15	25-32

Marvel Legends, Wonder Man, Series 11, Toy Biz, $8 MIP.

Storm (with long hair)	8	12-15
Ultimate Captain America	6	10-12

Series 9

Bullseye	4	10
Bullseye (variant)	4-6	12-15
Deathlok	4	10-12
Dr. Strange	4	10-12
Green Hulk (variant)	6-8	14-18
Grey Hulk	4	10
Nightcrawler	4	12-14
Professor X	4	10
War Machine	6-8	13-16

16" deluxe figure
Galactus (pieced together from individually-packed parts
   from each Series 9 MIP figure) Loose only: $45-55

Series 10

1st Appearance Spider-Man	4	10-12
Angel	4-6	12-14
Angel (X-Factor; variant)	8-10	18-25
Black Panther	4	8-10
Cyclops	4	8-10
Cyclops (X-Factor; variant)	6-8	16-22
Mr. Sinister	4	10
Mystique	4	10
Omega Red	4	10-12

16" deluxe figure
Sentinel (pieced together from individually-packed parts from each Series
   10 MIP figure) Loose only: $53-60

Series 11

1st Appearance Thing	3	8
Iron Man, Hulk Buster	6	12-15

Marvel Legends, Bishop (bald headed variant), Series 12, Toy Biz, $28 MIP.

Marvel Legends, Iron Fist (red costume variant), Series 12, Toy Biz, $30 MIP.

Marvel Legends, Sasquatch (orange/red fur), Series 12, Toy Biz, $12 MIP.

Marvel Legends, X-23 (black costume), Series 12, Toy Biz, $28 MIP.

Marvel Legends, X-23 (purple costume), Series 12, Toy Biz, $12 MIP.

Marvel Legends, Apocalypse, Series 12, Toy Biz, $48 (loose only).

Logan	4	10-12
Logan (variant)	8-10	20-25
Scarlet Witch	12-15	26-30
Taskmaster	4-6	12
Ultron	4-6	12
Vengeance	4	10
Wonder Man	3	8
Wonder Man (variant)	10-12	22-28

Series 12

Astonishing X-Men Wolverine (masked)	4	10
Astonishing X-Men Wolverine (unmasked, variant)	6-8	13-17
Bishop (with long hair)	4-6	10-12
Bishop (bald headed variant)	10-12	23-28
Iron Fist (green costume)	4-6	10-12
Iron Fist (red costume variant)	10-12	24-30
Maestro	4-6	10
Sasquatch (orange/red fur)	4-6	10-12
Sasquatch (white fur variant)	10-12	22-26
X-23 (purple costume)	4-6	10-12
X-23 (black costume variant)	10-12	22-28

16" deluxe figure

Apocalypse (pieced together from individually-packed parts from each
Series 12 MIP figure) Loose only: $45-48

Boxed Sets

Fantastic Four	15-20	35-40
Fantastic Four (variant)	35-40	80-85
Sinister Six	26-30	70-75
Urban Legends	12-15	20-25
X-Men Legends	12-15	20-25

Marvel Selects, Spider-Man v. Doctor Octopus, Toy Biz/Diamond Select, $18 MIP.

MASK Condor, Series 1, Kenner, 1985, $50 MISB.

Marvel Selects, Spider-Man v. Doctor Octopus, Toy Biz/Diamond Select, $18 MIP.

Marvel Selects, Thanos, Toy Biz/Diamond Select, $22 MIP.

Marvel Selects
(Toy Biz/Diamond Select, 2002-Present)

Black Cat	12-15	32-38
Black Widow	8-10	13-16
Captain America	8-10	13-16
Carnage	10	14-18
Dr. Doom	10-12	18-20
Elektra	8-10	13-16
(Ultimate) Gray Hulk	20-22	45-50
Green Goblin	8-10	20-22
(Ultimate) Iron Man	15-18	25-30
Phoenix	10	15-18
Phoenix (chase, "fiery")	10-12	16-20
Punisher	10-12	22-25
Spider-Man	8-10	14-18
Spider-Man (black costume)	8-10	14-18
(Ultimate) Spider-Man versus Doc Ock	8-10	14-18
Thanos	12-14	22
Thor	8	12-14
(Ultimate) Venom	10-12	16-18
White Queen	8-10	13-16
White Queen (chase, "clear")	10	14-16
(Ultimate) Wolverine	10	14-16
Wolverine: Days of Future Past	8-10	12-14
Wolverine: Origins	8-10	14-16

M.A.S.K.
(Kenner, 1985-88)

Series 1 (1985)

Boulder Hill	55-65	100 (150-175+ MISB)
Condor	15-20	30 (50+ MISB)
Firecracker	30	45 (75+ MISB)
Gator	20-22	35-40 (65+ MISB)

MASK Condor, Series 1, Kenner, 1985, $50 MISB.

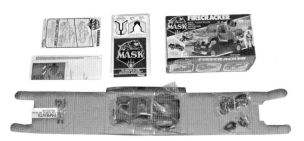

MASK Firecracker, Series 1, Kenner, 1985, $75 MISB.

MASK Switchblade, Series 1, Kenner, 1985, $120 MISB.

MASK Outlaw, Series 3, Kenner, 1986, $95 MISB.

Jackhammer	35-40	60 (85-90+ MISB)
Piranha	25-30	45 (65-75+ MISB)
Rhino	55-65	75-80 (125-135+ MISB)
Thunderhawk	40	60 (100+ MISB)
Switchblade	35-40	60 (110-120+ MISB)

UK exclusives; boxed

T-Bob and Scott Trakker	15-20	35-40 (50+ MISB)

Series 2 (1986)

Firefly	15-20	40
Hurricane	20-25	45
Outlaw	45-50	85-95
Raven	25-28	50
Slingshot	25	50
Stinger	25-30	45-50
Vampire	15-18	35-40
Volcano	30-35	55-65

Series 3 (1987): M.A.S.K. Racing Series

Note: On the cartoon show, there was a new race highlighting every episode, and these were fantastic toys. Mint in Sealed Box samples command some high prices.

Billboard Blast	15-20	45-50
Bulldog	30-35	55-65
Bullet	15-18	35-40
Buzzard	25-30	55-65
Collector, The	20-25	45
Goliath	65-70	120+
Iguana	15	35-40
Manta	20-25	50-55
Meteor	30-35	70-75+
Pit Stop Catapult	15-20	45-50
Razorback	35	65+
Wildcat	15-20	40-45

Series Four (1987-88): M.A.S.K. Split Seconds

Note: Each vehicle split into two parts, and each package came with a driver and a "clone"—a "splitting image." MISB samples are ridiculously expensive.

Afterburner	35	75+
Barracuda	35-40	80-85+
Detonator	40-45	100+
Dynamo	20-25	45+
Fireforce	38-40	100+
Skybolt	40-45	110+
Stiletto	40-45	100+
Vandal	18-20	40-45
Wolfbeast	40-45	120+

Series Five (1988): M.A.S.K. Laser Command

Note: These were the last vehicle and figures produced for the line.

Hornet and Ratfang	65-75	110 (160-175+ MISB)

McDonaldland

(Remco, 1976)

Note: Probably the best action figures Remco ever made—a company famous for crafting low-budget, low-detailed, and uninteresting licensed and unlicensed figures. These figures are fun, well-constructed, and are *very* popular with action figure collectors especially MOC.

Figures, 8"

Big Mac	29-32	65-75
Captain Crook	20-25	36-40
Grimace	30-35	75-85
Hamburglar	15-18	28-32
Mayor McCheese	30-35	65-75
Professor	20-25	35-38
Ronald McDonald	25-35	65-75

Playsets

McDonaldland (very difficult to find mint, loose, and complete or MIB/ MISB)	150-165	(240+ MISB)

McDonaldland 8" figures in clockwise order: Hamburglar ($32 MIP), Ronald McDonald ($75 MIP), Captain Crook ($40 MIP), Professor ($38 MIP); Remco, 1976.

Micronauts
(Mego, 1976-80)

Regular Micronauts figures, boxed

Andromeda	12-15	25-30
Baron Karza	20-22	40-45
Biotron	12-15	25-30
Force Commander	10-12	25-30
Giant Acroyear	12-15	25-30
Megas	10-12	25-30
Microtron	15	45-50
Nemesis Robot	15	30-35
Oberon	20	45-50
Phobos Robot	12	25-30

Regular Micronauts figures, carded

Acroyear	10	20
Acroyear II	15	30
Galactic Defender	15	30
Galactic Warrior	12	25
Pharoid with Time Chamber	18	35
Space Glider	15	30
Time Traveller (solid or clear plastic)	15	30

Alien Invaders, figures

Antron	25-32	100-110
Centaurus	50-55	200
Kronos	35-40	200
Lobros	35-40	200
Membros	20-25	100
Repto	20-25	100

Alien Invaders, vehicles

Alphatron	8-12	15-20
Betatron	8-12	15-20

Gammatron	8-12	15-20
Hornetriod	20-25	40-45
Hydra	7-12	20-25
Mobile Exploration Lab	20-25	35-40
Solarion	15-22	30-35
Star Searcher	15-22	40-45
Taurion	15-18	25-30
Terraphant	20-25	40-45

Micropolis playsets

Galactic Command Center	40	95
Interplanetary Headquarters	40	95
Mega City	40	95
Microrail City	40	95

Playsets

Astro Station	25	50
Rocket Tubes	45	90
Stratstation	30	65

Vehicles

Aquatron	10-12	20
Battle Cruiser	30-35	60-65
Crater Cruncher (with Time Traveller)	15-18	35-40
Galactic Cruiser	15	35
Hydro Copter	10	25
Neon Orbiter	6-8	20
Photon Sled	10-12	25
Rhodium Orbiter	10-12	30
Thorium Orbiter	10-12	25
Ultrasonic Scooter (with Time Traveller)	15	45
Warp Racer (with Time Traveller)	15	45

Planet of the Apes
(Mego, 1973-75)

Figures, 8"

Astronaut (boxed)	50	250
Astronaut (carded)	50	100
Astronaut Burke (boxed)	50	250
Astronaut Burke (carded)	50	100
Astronaut Verdon (boxed)	50	250
Astronaut Verdon (carded)	50	125
Cornelius (boxed)	40	200
Cornelius (carded)	40	100
Dr. Zaius (boxed)	40	200
Dr. Zaius (carded)	40	100
Galen (boxed)	40	200
Galen (carded)	40	100
General Urko (boxed)	50	250
General Urko (carded)	50	250
General Ursus (boxed)	50	250
General Ursus (carded)	50	250
Soldier Ape (boxed)	50	250
Solider Ape (carded)	50	200
Zira (boxed)	30	200
Zira (carded)	30	100

Accessories

Action Stallion	50	100
Battering Ram	20	40
Dr. Zaius' Throne	20	40
Jail	20	40

Playsets

Forbidden Zone Trap	90	200 (310+ MISB)
Fortress	85	200 (275-280+ MISB)
Treehouse	75	200 (300+ MISB)
Village	85	200 (300+ MISB)

Secret Wars, Doctor Doom, Series 1, Mattel, 1984-85, $20 MIP.

Vehicles

Catapault and Wagon	75	150 (200+ MISB)

Secret Wars
(Mattel, 1984-85)

Series 1, 4" figures

Note: Special three-packs sell for ridiculous amounts of money, and should be handled with the utmost care!

Captain America	8-10	20-25
Doctor Doom	8-10	15-20
Doctor Octopus	8-10	15-20
Iron Man	8-10	20-25
Kang the Conqueror	6-8	10-12
Magneto	6-8	10-12
Spider-Man	8-10	22-28+
Wolverine	12-15	35-45+
Wolverine (black claws)	35-40	120-135+

Series 2

Baron Zemo	8-10	20-25
Daredevil	8-10	25-30
Falcon	20-25	45-55+
Hobgoblin	20-25	45-55+
Spider-Man (black costume)	15-20	35-45+

Foreign Releases (1985)

Constrictor	45-50	100+
Electro	35-40	90+
Iceman	35-40	90+

Vehicles/Accessories

Doom Chopper	20-25	60+
Doom Chopper (with Doctor Doom)	25-30	130+
Doom Cycle	10-12	18
Doom Cycle (with Doctor Doom)	12-15	25

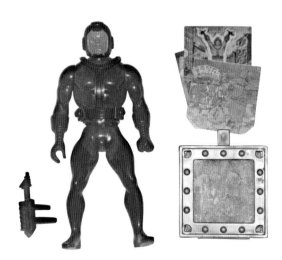

Secret Wars, Kang the Conqueror, Series 1, Mattel, 1984-85, $12 MIP.

Secret Wars, Wolverine (black claws), Series 1, Mattel, 1984-85, $135 MIP.

Secret Wars, Spider-Man in black costume, Series 2, Mattel, 1984-85, $45 MIP.

Secret Wars, Doom Roller, Mattel, 1984-85, $20 MIP.

Doom Roller	10-12	20
Doom Star Glider (with Kang)	10-12	25
Marvel Super Heroes Freedom Fighter Playset	12-15	40-50
Marvel Super Villains Tower of Doom Playset	12-15	40-50
Star Dart Glider (with Black Spider-Man)	20-25	50+
Turbo Copter	20-25	50
Turbo Copter (with Captain America)	25-30	100+
Turbo Cycle	8	10-12
Turbo Cycle (with Captain America)	15	50+

Silver Hawks

(Kenner, 1986)

Good Guys (1st and 2nd series; 6" figures)

Bluegrass (with Side Man)	6-8	15-20
Bluegrass (with Hot Licks)	8-10	20-25
Condor (with Jet Stream)	6-8	15-20
Copper Kidd (with May-Day)	6-8	15-20
Copper Kidd (with Laser Disks)	15-20	25-35
Flashback (with Backlash)	6-8	15-20
Hotwing (with Gyro)	6-8	15-20
Quicksilver (with Tallyhawk)	12-15	20-25+
Quicksilver (with Sonic Suit)	20-25	40+
Stargazer (with Sly-Bird)	6-8	15-20
Steelheart (with Rayzor)	12-15	20-25
Steelwill (with Stronghold)	12-15	20-25
Steelwill (with Laser Spark)	20-25	40+

Bad Guys (1st and 2nd series; 6" figures)

Buzz Saw (with Shredator)	6-8	15-20
Hardware (with Prowler)	6-8	15-20
Mo-Lec-U-Lar (with Volt-Ure)	6-8	15-20
Mon-Star (with Sky Shadow)	12	15-20
Mon-Star (with Laser Lance)	20-25	40+
Mumbo-Jumbo (with Airshock)	6-8	15-20
Windhammer (with Tuning Fork)	6-8	15-20

Vehicles/Accessories

Hawkhaven Stronghold	100	175+
Maraj	35-40	60+
Super Attack Bird Sky Shadow	15-20	40+
Super Attack Bird Stronghold	15-20	30+
Super Attack Bird Tallyhawk	15-20	30+

Simpsons, The
(Mattel, 1990)

Figures, 5"

Bart	6-8	15-20
Bartman	6-8	15-20
Homer	6-8	15-20
Lisa	12-15	35-40+
Maggie	12-15	35-40+
Marge	8-10	25-30+
Nelson	6-8	15-20
Simpsons Sofa and Boob Tube	15-18	30-35+

Simpsons, The
(Playmates, 2000-04)

Series 1 (Figures, 5")

Bart	6	20
Grandpa	10	30
Homer	8	20
Krusty	10	30
Lisa	10	30
Mr. Burns	10	20

Series 2

Barney	6	20
Chief Wiggum	6	20
Ned Flanders	6	20

Pin Pal Homer	6	20
Smithers	5	15
Sunday Best Bart	3	10

Series 3

Kamp Krusty Bart	5	9
Milhouse	5	10
Moe	7	15
Nelson	5	10
Otto	5	10
Sunday Best Homer	5	9

Series 4

Casual Homer	5	10
Groundskeeper Willie	5	10
Itchy and Scratchy	5	10
Lenny	5	10
Patty	5	10
Ralph Wiggum	5	10

Series 5

Bartman	5	10
Bumble Bee Man	6	12
Captain McCallister	5	10
Kent Brockman	5	10
Martin	5	10
Sideshow Mel	5	10

Series 6

Bleeding Gums Murphy	5	10
Carl	4	8
Dr. Hibbert	5	10
Isotopes Mascot Homer	5	10
Professor Frink	5	10
Snake	5	10

Simpsons, Left to right: Edna Krabappel ($8 MIP), Dolph ($10 MIP), and Officer Marge ($8 MIP), Series 7, Playmates.

Simpsons, Daredevil Bart, Series 8, Playmates, $8 MIP.

Simpsons, Kearney, Series 8, Playmates, $8 MIP.

Simpsons, Superintendent Chalmers, Series 8, Playmates, $8 MIP.

Simpsons, Busted Krusty the Clown and Prison Sideshow Bob, Series 9, Playmates, $8 MIP each.

Series 7

Cletus	5	10
Dolph	5	10
Hans Moleman	4	8
Mrs. Krabappel	4	8
Officer Lou	4	8
Officer Marge	4	8

Series 8

Daredevil Bart	4	8
Kearney	4	8
Ragin' Willie	4	8
Sherri and Terri	4	8
Superintendent Chalmers	4	8
Uter	4	8

Series 9

Busted Krusty the Clown	4	8
Disco Stu	4	8
Prison Sideshow Bob	4	8
Rod and Todd Flanders	4	8
Sunday Best Grandpa	4	8

Series 10

Hank Scorpio	5	10
Marvin Monroe	5	10
Resort Smithers	4	8
Scout Leader Flanders	4	8
Stonecutter Homer	4	8
Sunday Best Marge and Maggie	4	8
Wendell	4	8

Series 11

Blue Haired Lawyer	4	8
Gil	4	8
Kirk VanHouten	4	8

Larry Burns	4	8
Plow King Barney	4	8
Rainer Wolfcastle	4	8

Series 12

Database	4	8
Don Vittorio	4	8
Luann VanHouten	4	8
Moe (re-release)	4	8
Mr. Burns (re-release)	4	8
Mr. Largo	4	8
Mr. Plow Homer	4	8
Number 1	4	8

Series 13

Dr. Stephen Hawking	10	12
Freddy Quimby	4	8
Helen Lovejoy	4	8
Louie	4	8
Princess Kasmir	4	8
Tuxedo Krusty	4	8

Series 14

Legs	4	8
Luigi	4	8
Ms. Botz	4	8
Ms. Hoover	4	8
Raphael	4	8
Willie in Kilt	4	8

Series 15

Brandine	4	8
Comic Book Guy	4	8
Deep Space Homer	4	8
Octuplets	4	8
Manjula	4	8

Series 16

Agnes	4	8
Artie Ziff	4	8
Ben and Gary	4	8
Brain Freeze Bart	4	8
Doug	4	8
Evil Homer	4	8

Celebrity Series

Brad Goodman	4	8
Fat Tony	4	8
Herb Powell	4	8
Lionel Hutz	4	8
Troy McClure	4	8

Exclusive figures

All-Star Voices two-pack #1 (Toys 'R Us)	10	20
All-Star Voices two-pack #2 (Toys 'R Us)	10	20
Barney Gumble (Target, Wave 1)	7	12
Be-Sharp Apu (Playmates mail-in)	12	20+
Be-Sharp Barney (Playmates mail-in)	12	20+
Be-Sharp Homer (Playmates mail-in)	15-18	40+
Be-Sharp Skinner (Playmates mail-in)	12	20+
Bongo Comics 3-pack (Playmates)	9	18
Convention Comic Book Guy (Toyfare)	15	30
Cooder (Playmates mail-in)	12	25
Evil Krusty Doll (Diamond, talking)	10	20
Family Christmas (Toys 'R Us)	20	40
Family New Years (Toys 'R Us)	10	20
High School Prom (Diamond)	10	20
Homer Simpson (Target, Wave 1)	10	20
KBBL Radio (Diamond)	10	20
Llewellyn Sinclair (Playmates mail-in)	12	25
Lunar Base Environment (Diamond)	10	20

Simpsons, Military Antique Shop, Playmates, $16 MIP.

Simpsons, Springfield DMV, Playmates, $16 MIP.

Mainstreet Environment (Toys 'R Us)	20	40
Moe Szyslak (Target, Wave 2)	7	12
Moe's Tavern Environment (Diamond)	10	20
Mr. Burns (Target, Wave 1)	7	12
Pin Pal Moe (Toyfare)	10	20
Pin Pal Mr. Burns (Toyfare)	15	20
Radio Active Homer (Toyfare)	35	100+
Treehouse of Horror I (Toys 'R Us)	25	50
Treehouse of Horror II (Toys 'R Us)	25	50
Treehouse of Horror III (Toys 'R Us)	20	40
Treehouse of Horror IV (Toys 'R Us)	15	25
Treehouse of Horror (Toys 'R Us)	20	50

Environments (Playsets)

Aztec Theater	8	16
Bart's Treehouse	10	20
Bowl-A-Rama	10	20
Burns Manor	8	15
Comic Book Shop	10	20
Court Room	8	15
Doctor's Office	8	15
First Church of Springfield	10	20
Krusty Burger	10	20
Krustylu Studios	10	20
Kwik-E-Mart	8	20
Living Room	10	40
Military Antique Shop	8	16
Noiseland Arcade	10	20
Nuclear Power Plant	10	40
Nuclear Power Plant Lunch Room	8	16
Police Station	10	20
Retirement Castle	10	20
Simpson's Family Kitchen	10	20
Springfield DMV	8	16

Spawn, Overtkill, Series 1, McFarlane Toys, $20 MIP.

Springfield Elementary	10	20
Springfield Elementary School Cafeteria	10	20
Town Hall	10	20

Spawn
(McFarlane Toys, 1994-present)

Series 1 (1994, "Todd Toys" packaging)

Figures

Clown (clown head)	6	20
Clown (monster head)	6	10
Clown (Kay Bee exclusive)	3	10
Medieval Spawn	5	20
Medieval Spawn (Kay Bee exclusive)	5	15
Overtkill	7	20
Overtkill (Kay Bee exclusive, 1996)	3	12
Spawn (full mask)	5	25
Spawn (unmasked, "Hamburger Head")	15	40
Spawn (Kay Bee exclusive, 1995)	10	30
Spawn (Club exclusive, blue body, 1997)	8	20
Spawn (Club exclusive, green body, 1997)	8	20
Spawn (Diamond exclusive)	45	120
Spawn (Spawn #50 premium, "Worm Head," 1996)	50	150
Tremor (dark green costume)	8	15
Tremor (orange skin)	5	15
Tremor (Kay Bee exclusive)	3	12
Violator	5	20
Violator (chrome card)	8	20
Violator (Club exclusive, 1997)	8	20
Violator (green card)	5	15
Violator (Kay Bee exclusive, 1996)	4	12
Violator (mail-away, 1995)	20	75
Violator (red card)	5	15

Spawn, Tremor (orange skin), Series 1, McFarlane Toys, $15 MIP.

Spawn, Violator, Series 1, McFarlane Toys, $20 MIP.

Series 2 (1995)

Angela	5	25
Angela (Club exclusive, blue, 1997)	8	20
Angela (Club exclusive, pewter, 1997)	8	20
Angela (gold headpiece, gold and costume)	20	50
Angela (Kay Bee exclusive, 1997)	3	12
Angela (McFarlane Toy Collector's Club exclusive, 1996)	12	35
Angela (silver headpiece with silver and blue costume)	10	25
Badrock (blue)	10	25
Badrock (red pants)	3	12
Chapel (blue/black pants)	6	20
Chapel (khaki pants)	3	12
Commando Spawn	7	20
Malebolgia	30	60
Pilot Spawn (black costume)	8	20
Pilot Spawn (Kay Bee exclusive, 1997)	3	12
Pilot Spawn (white "Astronaut Spawn")	5	15

Series 3 (1995)

Cosmic Angela	5	15
Cosmic Angela (McFarlane Collector's Club exclusive, 1997)	5	15
Curse, The	5	15
Curse, The (McFarlane Collector's Club exclusive, 1997)	5	15
Future Spawn	5	15
Ninja Spawn	7	15
Ninja Spawn (McFarlane Collector's Club exclusive, 1997)	5	15
Redeemer	5	15
Redeemer (McFarlane Collector's Club exclusive, 1997)	5	15
Spawn II	10	15

Spawn II (McFarlane Collector's Club exclusive, 1997)	5	15
Vertebreaker	10	25
Vertebreaker (gray or black body)	5	15
Vertebreaker (McFarlane Collector's Club exclusive, 1997)	5	15
Violator II	10	20
Violator II (McFarlane Collector's Club exclusive, 1997)	5	15

Series 4 (1996)

Clown II (black guns)	6	20
Clown II (neon orange guns)	3	12
Cy-Gor (gold trim)	4	15
Cy-Gor (purple trim)	4	15
Cy-Gor (target exclusive)	5	15
Exo-Skeleton Spawn (black and gray exoskeleton)	5	20
Exo-Skeleton Spawn (Target exclusive, 1997)	5	15
Exo-Skeleton Spawn (light gray bones, white costume)	8	20
Future Spawn (red-trimmed)	10	15
Maxx (FAO Schwarz exclusive)	15	40
Maxx (with black Isz)	15	40
Maxx (with white Isz)	10	35
Shadowhawk (black with silver trim)	4	15
Shadowhawk (gold with gray trim)	3	10
She Spawn (black mask)	5	20
She Spawn (red mask)	5	20

Series 5 (1996)

Nuclear Spawn (green skin)	3	10
Nuclear Spawn (orange skin)	4	15
Overtkill II (gray trim)	5	15
Overtkill II (gold trim)	5	15
Tremor II (orange with red blood)	5	15

Tremor II (purple with green blood)	5	15
Vandalizer (FAO Schwarz exclusive)	10	25
Vandalizer (gray skinned with black trim)	3	10
Vandalizer (tan skinned with brown trim)	3	10
Viking Spawn	5	25
Widow Maker (black and red outfit)	5	15
Widow Maker (purple and rose outfit)	8	20

Series 6 (1996)

Alien Spawn (black with white)	5	15
Alien Spawn (white with black)	3	10
Battleclad Spawn (black costume)	5	20
Battleclad Spawn (tan sections)	4	12
Chameleon Spawn	4	12
Freak, The (purplish flesh)	3	10
Freak, The (tan flesh)	5	15
Sansker (black and yellow)	3	10
Sansker (brown and tan)	5	15
Superpatriot (metal-blue arms and legs)	3	10
Superpatriot (silver arms and legs)	3	10
Tiffany The Amazon (green trim)	5	15
Tiffany The Amazon (McFarlane Collector's Club exclusive)	8	25
Tiffany The Amazon (red trim)	5	15

Series 7 (1997)

Crutch (green goatee)	5	15
Crutch (purple goatee)	3	10
Mangler, The	5	15
No-Body	5	15
Sam And Twitch	5	15
Scourge	5	15
Spawn III (with owl and bat)	8	25
Spawn III (with wolf and bat)	8	25
Zombie Spawn	3	10

Series 8 (1997)

Curse Of The Spawn	5	15
Gate Keeper	4	12
Grave Digger	4	12
Renegade	4	12
Rotarr	4	12
Sabre	4	12

Series 9—Manga Spawn (1997)

Goddess, The	4	12
Manga Clown	4	12
Manga Curse	4	12
Manga Ninja Spawn	4	12
Manga Spawn	5	15
Manga Violator	4	12

Series 10—Manga Spawn II (1998)

Cyber Tooth	4	15
Manga Cyber Violator	4	8
Manga Dead Spawn	4	8
Manga Freak	4	8
Manga Overtkill	4	8
Manga Samurai Spawn	4	8

Series 11—The Dark Ages (1998)

Horrid, The	3	8
Ogre, The	5	15
Raider, The	3	8
Skull Queen	4	12
Spawn The Black Knight	5	15
Spellcaster	4	15

Series 12 (1998)

Bottomline	5	15
Creech, The	5	20
Cy-gor II	5	25

Spawn, Mandarin Spawn, Series 14: Dark Ages II, McFarlane Toys, 1999, $15 MIP.

Spawn, Gray Thunder, Series 15: Techno Spawn, McFarlane Toys, 1999, $10 MIP.

Heap, The	5	15
Reanimated Spawn	5	15
Spawn IV	5	15
Top Gun	5	15

Series 13—Curse of the Spawn (1999)

Curse Of The Spawn II	5	10
Desiccator	7	12
Hatchet	5	10
Jessica Priest And Mr. Obersmith	5	10
Medusa	5	10
Raenius	5	10
Zeus	5	10

Series 14—Dark Ages II (1999)

Iguantus and Tuskadon	5	15
Mandarin Spawn	5	15
Necromancer, The	5	15
Spawn The Black Heart	5	15
Tormentor	5	15
Viper King, The	5	15

Series 15—Techno Spawn (1999)

Code Red	5	15
Cyber Spawn	5	15
Grey Thunder	3	10
Iron Express	3	10
Steel Trap	3	10
Warzone	3	10

Series 16—Nitro Riders (2000)

After Burner	3	10
Eclipse 5000	3	10
Flash Point	3	10
Green Vapor	3	10

Series 17—Spawn Classics (2001)

Al Simmons II	3	8
Clown III	3	8
Malebolgia II	3	8
Medieval Spawn II	5	15
Spawn V	5	15
Tiffany II	5	15

Series 18—Interlink 6 (2001)

Note: All 6 robots combine to form a larger robot.

HD-1	3	10
LA-6	3	10
LL-4	3	10
RA-5	3	10
RL-3	3	10
TS-2	3	10

Series 19—Dark Ages Spawn: The Samurai Wars (2001)

Dojo	5	10
Jackal Assassin	5	10
Jyaaku The Nightmare	7	12
Lotus The Angel Warrior	5	10
Samurai Spawn	5	10
Scorpion Assassin	5	10

Series 20—Spawn Classics II (2001)

Clown IV	5	10
Domina	5	10
Medieval Spawn III	5	10
Overtkill III	5	10
Spawn VI	5	10
Violator III	5	10

Series 21—Alternate Realities (2002)

Alien Spawn II	7	12
Pirate Spawn	7	12

Raven Spawn	7	12
She Spawn II	7	12
Spawn VII	7	12
Wings Of Redemption Spawn	10	20

Series 22—Dark Ages Spawn: The Viking Age (2002)

Berserker The Troll	7	12
Bluetooth	7	12
Dark Raider	7	12
Skullsplitter	7	12
Spawn The Bloodaxe	7	12
Spawn The Bloodaxe and Thunderhoof	10	22
Valkerie	7	12

Series 23—Mutations (2003)

Al Simmons	5	10
Kin	5	10
Lilith	5	10
Malebolgia	5	10
Spawn	5	10
Warrior Lilith	5	10

Series 23.5—Spawn Reborn (2003)

Clown IV	5	10
Curse of the Spawn II	5	10
Domina	5	10
Raven Spawn	5	10
Redeemer	5	10
Wings of Redemption Spawn	5	10

Series 24—The Classic Comic Covers (2003)

Dark Ages (issue 23)	3	10
Hellspawn (issue 01)	3	10
Spawn (issue 39)	3	10
Spawn (issue 43)	3	10
Spawn (issue 64)	3	10

Spawn (issue 88)	3	10
Spawn (issue 109)	3	10

Series 25—The Classic Comic Covers II (2003)

Creech (from *Creech* issue 01)	3	10
Hellspawn (from *Hellspawn* issue 05)	3	10
Hellspawn (from *Hellspawn* issue 11)	3	10
Redeemer (issue 117)	3	10
Sam And Twitch (from *Sam and Twitch* issue 22)	3	10
Spawn (issue 95)	3	10

Series 26—The Art of Spawn (2004)

Spawn (issue 7)	5	10
Spawn (issue 8)	5	10
Spawn The Dark Ages (issue 1)	5	10
Spawn vs. Cy-Gor (issue 57)	5	10
The Curse (from the *Spawn Bible* one-shot)	5	10
Tiffany (issue 45)	5	10
Tremor (from the *Spawn Bible* one-shot)	5	10

Series 27—The Art of Spawn II (2004)

Clown 5	5	10
Spawn (issue 85)	5	10
Spawn (issue 86: Spawn vs. Al Simmons)	10	25
Spawn (issue 119)	5	10
Spawn (issue 131)	5	10
Vandalizer 2	5	10
Wanda 2	5	10

Series 28—Regenerated (2004/05)

Commando Spawn 2	5	10
Cyber Spawn 2	5	10
Grave Digger 2	5	10
Lotus Warrior Angel 2	5	10
Mandarin Spawn 2	5	10
Spawn vs. Urizen Deluxe Boxed Set	10	25
Zombie Spawn 2	5	10

Spider-Man: The New Animated Series, Shocker, Toy Biz, $15 MIP.

Spider-Man: The New Animated Series
(Toy Biz, 1994-96)

Figures, 5"

Alien Spider Slayer	3	8
Battle-Ravaged Spider-Man	3	10
Chameleon	4	12
Carnage	5	15
Carnage II	4	12
(Maximum) Carnage	4-5	15-18
Dr. Octopus	4	12
Green Goblin	5	15
Hobgoblin	4	12
Kingpin	5	15
Kraven	4	12
Lizard	5	15
Man-Spider	5	10
Morbius	4	12
Mysterio	3	12
Nick Fury	3	12
Peter Parker	5	15
Prowler	3	12
Punisher	3	12
Rhino	6	18-22
Scorpion	5	15
Shocker	4	15
Smythe	5	12
Spider-Man 2099	6	12
Spider-Man, Black Costume	3	12
Spider-Man, "multi-jointed"	3	15
Spider-Man, Octo	5	10
Spider-Man, Six-Armed	3	12
Spider-Man with Spider Armor	3	15

Spider-Man: The New Animated Series, Spider-Man black costume, Toy Biz, $12 MIP.

Spider-Man: The New Animated Series, Spider-Man with Web Cannon, Toy Biz,
$18 MIP.

Spider-Man: The New Animated Series, Venom, Toy Biz, $15 MIP.

Spider-Man with Web Cannon	9	18
Spider-Man, with Web Parachute	8	15
Spider-Man with Web Racer	5	15
Spider-Man with Web Shooter	5	15
Spider-Sense Spider-Man Symbiotic Venom Attack	3	12
Tombstone	5	10
Venom	4	15
Venom II	3	12
Vulture	5	15

10" figures, deluxe

Note: Spider-Man 10" figures sell for approximately $7-8 ea. loose, while MIB specimens have a secondary-market value of $15 ea.

Vehicles

Hobgoblin Wing Bomber	10	25
Smythe Battle Chair Attack Vehicle	15	40
Spider-Man Wheelie Cycle	7	15
Spider-Man's Cycle (radio-controlled)	15	30
Tri-Spider Slayer	10	25

Star Trek

(Mego, 1974-80)

Figures, 8"

Andorian	300	650+
Captain Kirk	20-25	50-60
Cheron	85-90	175-185+
Dr. McCoy	35	75
Gorn	80	180
Klingon	25-30	50
Lt. Uhura	50	135-150+
Mr. Spock	20-25	50-60
Mugato	275	500+
Neptunian	100	225+

Star Trek, Dr. McCoy, 8" figure, Mego, 1974, $75 MIP.

Romulan	550-600	1000+
Scotty	35-40	80-85+
Talos	275	500+
The Keeper	75	175+

Playsets

Mission to Gamma VI	300	725+
U.S.S. Enterprise Bridge playset	100+	275-300+

Star Trek, Classic Movie Figures
(Playmates, 1995)

Figures, 5"

Admiral Kirk	4-6	8
Commander Kruge	4-6	8
Commander Spock	4-6	8
Dr. McCoy	4-6	8
General Chang	4-6	8
Khan	6-8	12-15
Lt. Saavik	4-6	8
Lt. Sulu	4-6	8
Lt. Uhura	4-6	8
Martia	6-8	12-15

Star Trek, Deep Space Nine
(Playmates, 1994-95)

Series 1 (Figures, 5")

Chief Miles O'Brien	3-4	6-8
Commander Benjamin Sisko	3-4	6-8
Commander Gul Ducat	3-4	6-8
Dr. Julian Bashir	3-4	6-8
Lt. Jadzia Dax	3-4	6-8
Major Kira Nerys	3-4	6-8
Morn	3-4	6-8

Odo	3-4	6-8
Quark	3-4	6-8

Series 2

Captain Jean-Luc Picard	3-4	6-8
Chief Miles O'Brien, dress uniform	3-4	6-8
Chief Miles O'Brien, duty uniform	3-4	6-8
Commander Benjamin Sisko, dress uniform	3-4	6-8
Dr. Julian Bashir, duty uniform	3-4	6-8
Jake Sisko	3-4	6-8
Lt. Jadzia Dax, duty uniform	3-4	6-8
Lt. Thomas Riker	3-4	6-8
Q	3-4	6-8
Rom with Nog	3-4	6-8
Tosk	3-4	6-8
Vedek Bareil	3-4	6-8

Star Trek: First Contact
(Playmates, 1996)

Figures, 5"

Borg	4-6	8-10
Captain Jean-Luc Picard	4-6	8-10
Commander Deanna Troi	4-6	8-10
Commander William T. Riker	4-6	8-10
Dr. Beverly Crusher	4-6	8-10
Lily	4-6	8-10
Lt. Commander Geordi LaForge	4-6	8-10
Lt. Commander Data	4-6	8-10
Lt. Commander Worf	4-6	8-10
Picard in Starfleet Spacesuit	4-6	8-10
Zefram Cocrane	4-6	8-10

Figures, 9"

Data	8-10	15
Jean-Luc Picard	8-10	15

Jean-Luc Picard in 21st century outfit	8-10	15
William Riker	8-10	15
Zefram Cochrane	8-10	15

Star Trek, Generations
(Playmates, 1994)

Figures, 5"

Admiral James T. Kirk	3-4	6-8
B'Etor	3-4	6-8
Captain James T. Kirk in Spacesuit	3-4	6-8
Captain Jean-Luc Picard	3-4	6-8
Commander Deanna Troi	3-4	6-8
Dr. Beverly Crusher	3-4	6-8
Dr. Soran	3-4	6-8
Guinan	3-4	6-8
Lt. Commander Data	3-4	6-8
Lt. Commander Geordi LaForge	3-4	6-8
Lt. Commander William Riker	3-4	6-8
Lt. Commander Worf	3-4	6-8
Lt. Commander Worf in 19th Century Outfit	3-4	6-8
Lursa	3-4	6-8
Montgomery Scott	6-8	10-12
Pavel A. Chekov	6-9	10-12

Figures, 9"

Captain James T. Kirk	8-10	25-28
Captain Jean-Luc Picard	6-8	12-15
Lt. Commander Data	6-8	12-15
Lt. Commadner Geordi LaForge	6-8	12-15

Star Trek, Insurrection
(Playmates, 1998)

Figures, 5"

Captain Picard	5-6	12

Data	5-6	12
Geordi LaForge	5-6	12
William Riker	5-6	12
Worf	5-6	12

Figures, 9"

Anji	6-8	12-15
Counselor Troi	6-8	12-15
Data	6-8	12-15
Geordi LaForge	6-8	12-15
Jean-Luc Picard	6-8	12-15
Ru'Afo	6-8	12-15
William Riker	6-8	12-15
Worf	6-8	12-15

Star Trek, Mixed Sets
(Playmates, 1996-97)

Series 1 (Figures, 5")

Captain Jean-Luc Picard ("Tapestry" Picard; ltd. to 1701)	60-65	175+
Christine Chapel	5-6	10
Commander Benjamin Sisko	5-6	10
Grand Negus Zek	5-6	10
Janice Rand	5-6	10
Worf, Governor of H'Atoria	5-6	10

Series 2

Admiral William Riker	5-6	10
Captain Kirk, casual	5-6	10
Jem Haddar	5-6	10
Lt. Commander Worf	5-6	10
Lt. Natasha Yar ("Yesterday's Enterprise" Yar; ltd. to 1701)	55-60	150+
Security Chief Odo	5-6	10

Star Trek: The Motion Picture, Decker, Series 1, 3-3/4" figure, Mego, 1979, $18 MIP.

Series 3

Captain Christopher Pike	5-6	10
Elim Garak	5-6	10
Lt. Reginald Barclay		
("Projections" Barclay; ltd. to 3000)	45-50	$125+
Mr. Spock	5-6	10
Talosian Keeper	5-6	10
Vina, the Orion Slave Girl	8-12	25

Series 4

Captain Benjamin Sisko	5-6	10
Captain Kurn	5-6	10
Dr. Beverly Crusher		
("Generations" Crusher; ltd. to 10,000)	8-12	25-30+
Gorn Captain	5-6	10
Seska as Cardassian	5-6	10
Tom Paris Mutated	5-6	10

Series 5

Captain Kirk in Environmental Suit	5-6	10
Dr. McCoy in dress uniform		
("Journey to Babel"; ltd. to 10,000)	10-12	25-30+
Harry Mudd	5-6	10
Professor Data	5-6	10
The Mugatu	5-6	10

Star Trek: The Motion Picture

(Mego, 1979)

Series 1

3-3/4" Figures

Decker	5-6	15-18
Ilia	5-6	15-18
Kirk	5-6	15-18
McCoy	5-6	15-18

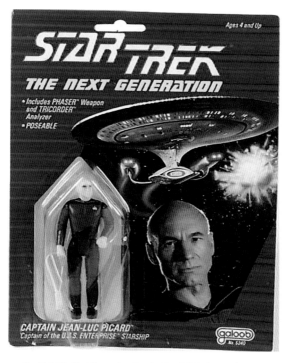

Star Trek: The Next Generation, Captain Picard, Galoob, 1988, $15 MIP.

Scotty	5-6	15-18
Spock	5-6	15-18

12" figures

Arcturian	45-50	125+
Decker	45-50	115+
Ilia	35-40	100+
Kirk	30-35	90+
Klingon	45-50	135+
Spock	35-40	90+

Series 2

3-3/4" Figures

Arcturian	75	150
Betelgeusian	75	150
Klingon	75	150
Megarite	75	150
Rigellian	75	150
Zaranite	75	150

Vehicles and Accessories

U.S.S. Enterprise Bridge	45	105

Star Trek: The Next Generation
(Galoob, 1988)

Series 1 (1988)

3-3/4" Figures

Captain Jean-Luc Picard	4-5	10-12
Commander William Riker	4-5	10-12
Data (many variations, i.e. "speckled" to "spotted")	4-5	10-12
Data (Blue-green face)	20-30	75-80
Geordi LaForge	4-5	10-12
Lt. Worf	4-5	10-12
Tasha Yar	4-5	10-12

Star Trek: The Next Generation, Borg, Series 1, Playmates, $8 MIP.

Star Trek: The Next Generation, Captain Jean-Luc Picard, Series 1, Playmates, $8 MIP.

Series 2 (1989)
Note: Sent to retailers who expressly ordered them, not as follow-up stock to Series 1, so these "aliens," like the original Mego Star Trek Aliens, were notoriously rare to obtain. Over the past five years, demand has decreased.

3-3/4" Figures

Antican	10-12	15-20
Ferengi	12-15	22-25
Q	12-15	22-25
Selay	10-12	15-20

Vehicles

Ferengi Fighter	22-25	30-35
Galileo Shuttlecraft	22-25	30-35
Phaser	15-20	25-30

Star Trek: The Next Generation
(Playmates, 1992-96)
Note: In recent years, ST:TNG MOC and MLC figures have plummeted in value (with the exception of the more premiere pieces) due to lack of movie and television support for the characters. Frequently, the more common figures from this series are sold in lots (again, carded or loose) for between $1-2 apiece (MLC) or $3-5 a piece (MOC). Of course, as soon as a media outlet is there to support these characters, their prices will rise accordingly.

Series 1 (Figures, 5")

Borg (w/ or w/out reversed image MOC)	3-4	6-8
Captain Jean-Luc Picard	3-4	6-8
Commander Riker	3-4	6-8
Counselor Deanna Troi (lavender outfit)	6-8	10-13
Ferengi (w/ or w/ out black trim on boots, w/ or w/out reversed image MOC)	3-4	6-8
Gowron the Klingon (w/ or w/ out gold trim on belt buckle)	5-6	10-12
Lt. Commander Data	3-4	6-8

Star Trek: The Next Generation, Klingon Warrior Worf, Series 2, Playmates, $8 MIP.

Star Trek: The Next Generation, Lieutenant (J.G.) Geordi LaForge, Series 2, Playmates, $8 MIP.

Lt. Commander Geordi La Forge		
(w/ and w/out removable visor)	3-4	6-8
Lt. Worf	3-4	6-8
Romulan	3-4	6-8

Series 2

Note: All Series 2 figures were released with promotionals packaged in MOC specimens—either a "Space Cap" resembling the defunct "pogs" of the early '90s, or a collectible trading card. Figures released with Space Caps were, at one time, highly collectible due to the limited run of these figures with Caps MOC. Further note that many of the Series 1 characters were re-released with either Space Caps or collectible gaming cards.

Admiral McCoy	3-4	6-8
Ambassador Spock	3-4	6-8
Benzite	3-4	6-8
Borg (with chrome arm)	3-4	6-8
Cadet Wesley Crusher	3-4	6-8
Captain Jean-Luc Picard (1st season uniform)	3-4	6-8
Captain Scott (Scotty)	3-4	6-8
Commander Sela	3-4	6-8
Commander William Riker	3-4	6-8
Counselor Deanna Troi (2nd season red uniform)	3-4	6-8
Dathon	3-4	6-8
Dr. Beverly Crusher	3-4	6-8
Guinan	2-3	4-5
K'Ehleyr	3-4	6-8
Klingon Warrior Worf	3-4	6-8
Locutus (Captain Jean-Luc Picard as Locutus)	3-4	6-8
Lore	3-4	6-8
Lt. Commander Geordi LaForge in dress uniform	3-4	6-8
Lt. Commander Data (1st season uniform)	3-4	6-8
Lt. Geordi Laforge	3-4	6-8
Lt. (JG) Worf (1st season red uniform)	3-4	6-8
Q, red shirt	3-4	6-8
Vorgon	3-4	6-8

*Star Trek: The Next Generation, Q in red Starfleet Uniform, Series 2, Playmates,
$8 MIP.*

Star Trek: The Next Generation, Vorgon, Series 2, Playmates, $8 MIP.

Star Trek: The Next Generation, Commander Riker as Malcorian, Series 3, Playmates, $8 MIP.

Series 3

Captain Jean-Luc Picard as Dixon Hill	3-4	6-8
Captain Picard as Romulan (from "Unification")	3-4	6-8
Captain Picard, red duty uniform	3-4	6-8
Commander Riker, Malcorian (from "First Contact")	3-4	6-8
Dr. Noonian Soong	3-4	6-8
Ensign Wesley Crusher	3-4	6-8
Esoqq Member of the Chalnoth race	12-15	20-25
Gowron in Ritual Klingon Attire	3-4	6-8
Hugh Borg	3-4	6-8
Lt. Barclay	3-4	6-8
Lt. Commander Data as Romulan (from "Unification")	3-4	6-8
Lt. Commander Data in dress uniform	3-4	6-8
Lt. Commander Data red "Redemption" Outfit	55+	125+
Lt. Commander Deanna Troi (6th season green uniform)	3-4	6-8
Lt. Commander Geordi LaForge (as Tarchannen III alien from "Identity Crisis")	3-4	6-8
Lt. Thomas Riker	15+	35-40+
Q in judge's robes	3-4	6-8
Worf in Starfleet rescue outfit (from "Birthright I and II")	3-4	6-8

Series 4

Ambassador Sarek	3-4	6-8
Captain Jean-Luc Picard as Locutus (metallic armor)	3-4	6-8
Captain Jean-Luc Picard (from "All Good Things")	3-4	6-8
Dr. Beverly Crusher, duty uniform	3-4	6-8
Dr. Noonian Soong	3-4	6-8
Ensign Ro Laren	3-4	6-8
Lt. Commander Data in 1940's attire	3-4	6-8
Lt. Commander Data in movie uniform (from *Generations*)	3-4	6-8

Star Trek: The Next Generation, Transporter, Playmates, $28 MIB.

Lt. Commander Geordi LaForge in movie uniform	3-4	6-8
Lt. Natasha Yar	3-4	6-8
Lt. Worf in Ritual Klingon Attire (metallic armor)	3-4	6-8
Lwaxana Troi	3-4	6-8
Nausicaan (from "Tapestry")	3-4	6-8

Series 5

Borg	3-4	6-8
Counselor Troi as Durango	3-4	6-8
Dr. Beverly Crusher in 1940's attire	3-4	6-8
Dr. Katherine Puylaski	3-4	6-8
Geordi LaForge	3-4	6-8
Lt. Geordi LaForge	3-4	6-8
Picard as Galen	3-4	6-8
Sheriff Worf	3-4	6-8
The Traveler	3-4	6-8
Vash	3-4	6-8

Multi-packs

Officers Set	10-12	20

Vehicles and Accessories

Borg Cube	40-50	60-65+
Bridge Playset	55-65	100-110+
Communicator	10-12	15-18
Enterprise D	10-12	15-20
Klingon Attack Cruiser	15-18	25-30
Klingon Bird of Prey	20-25	35-40+
Phaser	4-5	10-12
Phaser, Type 1	6-8	12-15
Shuttle Goddard	10-12	20-22
Transporter	10-15	25-28
Tricorder	20-22	40-50

Star Trek, Space Talk Series
(Playmates, 1995)

Figures, 5"

Borg	5-6	10
Picard	5-6	10
Q	5-6	10
Riker	5-6	10

Star Trek, Starfleet Academy
(Playmates, 1996)

Figures, 5"

Cadet Geordi LaForge	3-5	8-10
Cadet Jean-Luc Picard	3-5	8-10
Cadet William Riker	3-5	8-10
Cadet Worf	3-5	8-10

Star Trek: Voyager
(Playmates, 1995-96)

Figures, 5"

Captain Kathryn Janeway	3-5	10-12
Chatokay the Maquis	3-5	10-12
Commander Chatokay	3-5	10-12
Doctor	3-5	10-12
Ensign Harry Kim	3-5	10-12
Ensign Seska	3-5	10-12
Kazon	3-5	10-12
Kes the Ocampa	3-5	10-12
Lt. B'Elanna Torres	5-6	12-15
Lt. Carey	3-5	10-12
Lt. Tom Paris	3-5	10-12
Lt. Tuvok	3-5	10-12
Neelix the Telaxian	3-5	10-12

Torres as Klingon	3-5	10-12
Vidian	3-5	10-12

Vehicles

U.S.S. Voyager	15	30

Star Trek, Transporter Series
(Playmates, 1998)

Classic Series Figures, 5"

Kirk	3-5	10-12
McCoy	3-5	10-12
Scotty	3-5	10-12
Spock	3-5	10-12
Uhura	3-5	10-12

Next Generation Figures, 5"

Data	3-5	10-12
LaForge	3-5	10-12
Picard	3-5	10-12
Riker	3-5	10-12
Worf	3-5	10-12

Star Trek: Warp Factor
(Playmates, 1997-98)

Series 1

Note: The Series 1 action figures that came with "fuzzy tribbles" rather than the standard plastic ones are worth a bit more (2-3 dollars) on the secondary market.

Captain Benjamin Sisko	3-5	8-10
Captain Koloth	3-5	8-10
Chief Miles O'Brien	3-5	8-10
Constable Odo	3-5	8-10
Dr. Julian Bashir	3-5	8-10
Lt. Commander Jadzia Dax	3-5	8-10

Series 2

Captain Beverly Picard	3-5	8-10
Ilia Probe	3-5	8-10
Leeta the Dabo Girl	3-5	8-10
Sisko as a Klingon	3-5	8-10
Swarm Alien	3-5	8-10

Series 3

Cadet Beverly Howard Crusher	3-5	8-10
Cadet Data	3-5	8-10
Cadet Deanna Troi	3-5	8-10
Edith Keeler	3-5	8-10
Mr. Spock ("Mirror, Mirror")	3-5	8-10

Series 4

Andorian	3-5	8-10
Intendant Kira	3-5	8-10
Kang	3-5	8-10
Keiko O'Brien	3-5	8-10
Trelane	3-5	8-10

Series 5

Borg Queen	3-5	8-10
James Kirk	3-5	8-10
Mr. Spock ("City on the Edge of Forever")	3-5	8-10
Seven of Nine	3-5	8-10

Star Wars, Vintage Line

(Kenner, 1977-84)

(figures, 3-3/4"[approximate height – some are taller or shorter, but this is the 'basic' scale])

Star Wars

(Kenner, 1977)

Figures released on original 12-back cards—for ease of collecting, I have numbered all of the original "96" figures.

Left: Star Wars, Ben (Obi-Wan) Kenobi, Kenner, 1977, $300 MIP.

Right: Star Wars, Star Destroyer Commander, Kenner, 1980, $190 MIP.

Left: Star Wars, Jawa, Kenner, 1977, $200 MIP.

Right: Star Wars, Luke Skywalker (yellow hair), Kenner, 1977, $450 MIP.

Left: Star Wars, Princess Leia Organa, Kenner, 1977, $420 MIP.

Right: Star Wars, Stormtrooper, Kenner, 1977, $250 MIP.

1) Artoo-Detoo (R2-D2)	5-10	175
2) Ben (Obi-Wan) Kenobi (gray or white hair)*	15-20	300
3) Chewbacca (black or dark green)	15-20	200
Chewbacca (bowcaster variants;		
the green one is quite rare)	50 MLC	450+ MOC
4) Darth Vader*	15-25	410
5) Death Squad Commander		
(Star Destroyer Commander on later cards)	5-10	190
6) Han Solo (large head)	12-18	475
Han Solo (small head)	20-22	500+
7) Jawa**	10-12	200 (cloth cape)
8) Luke Skywalker* (yellow hair)	10-12	450
Luke Skywalker* (brown hair)	30-35	475
9) Princess Leia Organa	12-15	420
10) C-3PO (See-Threepio)	5-10	200
11) Sand People (Tusken Raider)	8-12	210
12) Stormtrooper/Imperial Stormtrooper	8-12	250

*Note: The three figures that came with light sabers (Ben Kenobi, Darth Vader, and Luke Skywalker) were released with double telescoping light sabers—light sabers that extended twice. These figures are quite rare and command prices ten to a hundred times the price of their regular mint, loose, complete counterparts. Luke (telescoping saber) sells for $185 loose complete and $3200-3500 MOC; the other two garner similar prices!

**The rarer variant of the Jawa is the version with a vinyl instead of a cloth cape. Beware of dealers offering Jawas with vinyl capes, as these are impossible to find and are usually repros. Try to have the vinyl caped Jawa authenticated by a reputable dealer prior to purchase. Actual vinyl-caped Jawas sell for more than $2000-2500 MOC, and $250+ for mint, loose and complete samples.

Star Wars
(Kenner, 1978/Early 1979; 20, 21-back cards)

13) Arfive-Defour (R5-D4)	5-10	200
14) Death Star Droid	8-10	160

Left: Star Wars, Hammerhead, Kenner, 1978, $185 MIP.

Right: Star Wars, Boba Fett, Kenner, 1978, $650 MIP.

Left: Star Wars, Snaggletooth, blue version released only with Sears Exclusive Cantina Adventure Playset, Kenner, 1978, $80-100 loose.

Right: Star Wars, Snaggletooth, red version, Kenner, 1978, $170 MIP.

Left: The Empire Strikes Back, AT-AT Driver, Kenner, 1980, $80 MIP.

Right: The Empire Strikes Back, Bespin Security Guard (white), Kenner, 1980, $50 MIP.

15) Greedo	8-12	200
16) Hammerhead	8-12	185
17) Luke Skywalker X-Wing Pilot	8-12	185
18) Power Droid	5-10	135
19) Snaggletooth*	8-12	170
20) Walrus Man	8-12	125
21) Boba Fett ** (available carded, but originally as a mail-away offer)	15-25 40-45 (mailer box)	650+

*Note: The Snaggletooth that was released MOC was the shorter maroon-costumed version of the character. The rare and quite expensive Sears Exclusive Cantina Adventure Playset (made of chipboard) included four denizens of the famous Creature Cantina: Greedo, Hammerhead, Walrusman, and Snaggletoth, but a *taller* Snaggletooth with a blue costume. This "blue" Snaggletooth is in high demand, commanding prices upwards of $80-100 and more.

** As one of the most popular Star Wars characters ever, Boba Fett—a bounty hunter who only spoke a total of 27 words in the entire original trilogy—has become a high-demand action figure. However, like the vinyl-caped Jawa (see #7), Boba Fett was *never* released with his "rocket-firing backpack" in *any* way to the general public. These figures only show up as Kenner prototypes—so beware of fakes! If you manage to track one down, have it verified by a reputable Star Wars dealer.

The Empire Strikes Back
(Kenner, 1980-1981; 31, 32, and 41-back cards)

22) AT-AT Commander	5-8	95
23) AT-AT Driver	5-10	80
24) Bespin Security Guard ("white")	10-12	50
25) Bespin Security Guard ("black")	10-12	60
26) Bossk (available carded, but originally as a mail-away offer)	5-8 30-35 (mailer box)	85 (MOC)
27) Dengar	5-8	80
28) FX-7 (Medical Droid)	5-8	80

Left: The Empire Strikes Back, Imperial Commander, Kenner, 1980, $50 MIP.

Right: The Empire Strikes Back, Rebel Soldier (Hoth Battle Gear), Kenner, 1980, $50 MIP.

The Empire Strikes Back, Imperial Stormtrooper (Hoth Battle Gear) a.k.a. Snowtroopers, Kenner, 1980, $95 MIP.

Left: The Empire Strikes Back, Yoda (orange snake), Kenner, 1980, $185 MIP.

Right: The Empire Strikes Back, Yoda (brown snake), Kenner, 1980, $185 MIP.

29) Han Solo (Bespin Outfit)	6-10	75
30) Han Solo (Hoth Battle Gear)	6-10	95
31) IG-88 (Bounty Hunter; silver and gray variations)	6-10	135
32) Imperial Commander (skinny and round head variations)	8-10	50
33) Imperial Stormtrooper (Hoth Battle Gear)	8-10	95
34) Lando Calrissian (teeth and no teeth variations)	6-10	75
35) Luke Skywalker (Bespin Fatigues; yellow and brown hair variations)	10-15	120
36) Leia Organa (Bespin Gown)	12-18	120
Leia Organa (gold/green neck variant)	15+	130+
37) Lobot	5-8	40
38) Princess Leia Organa (Hoth Outfit)	6-10	75
39) Rebel Commander	6-10	65
40) Rebel Solider (Hoth Battle Gear)	6-10	50
41) Two-Onebee (2-1B) (metallic and flat paint variants)	5-10	95
42) Ugnaught (purple and blue apron variations)	5-10	55
43) Yoda (orange and brown snake variations)	15-25	185

The Empire Strikes Back

(Kenner, 1981-1982; 45, 47, 48-back cards)

44) Artoo-Deeto (with Sensorscope)	7-10	60
45) 4-LOM (available carded, but originally as a mail-away offer)	10-12	25-30(mailer box) 110-120 (MOC)
46) Imperial Tie Fighter Pilot	8-10	85
47) Luke Skywalker (Hoth Battle Gear)	8-12	115
48) C-3PO (See-Threepio; with removable limbs)	5-10	55
49) (Twin-Pod) Cloud Car Pilot	10-12	75
50) Zuckuss	5-10	95

Left: Return of the Jedi, Bib Fortuna, Kenner, 1983, $35 MIP.

Right: Return of the Jedi, 8D8, Kenner, 1983, $55 MIP.

Left: Return of the Jedi, Klaatu, Kenner, 1983, $30 MIP.

Right: Return of the Jedi, Nikto, Kenner, 1983, $30 MIP.

Left: Return of the Jedi, Squid Head, Kenner, 1983, $50 MIP.

Right: Return of the Jedi, Weequay, Kenner, 1983, $45 MIP.

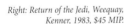

Return of the Jedi
(Kenner, 1983; 65, 66, 77, 79-back cards)

51) Admiral Ackbar (available carded, but originally as a mail-away offer)	5-10	30
52) Bib Fortuna (beware of red cloaked Bib Fortunas, as these were not readily available to the public)	6-10	30-35
53) Biker Scout	10-15	75-80
54) Chief Chirpa	8-12	40-45
55) 8D8	5-10	55
56) Emperor's Royal Guard	8-12	55
57) Gammorean Guard	5-10	25-30
58) General Madine	5-10	35-40
59) Klaatu	5-10	30
60) Klaatu (In Skiff Guard Outfit)	5-10	30
61) Lando Calrissian (Skiff Guard Disguise)	5-10	40-45
62) Logray (Ewok Medicine Man)	8-12	40
63) Luke Skywalker (Jedi Knight Outfit) (green lightsaber)	12-18	60+
Luke Skywalker (blue light saber)	25-40	110+
64) Nien Nunb (available carded, but originally as a mail-away offer)	5-10	15-20(mailer box) 50 (MOC)
65) Nitko	5-10	30
66) Princess Leia Organa (Boussh Disguise) 8-10	45	
67) Rebel Commando	5-10	35
68) Ree-Yees	5-10	25
69) Squid Head	6-10	50
70) Weequay	5-10	45

Return of the Jedi
(Kenner, 1984; 77, 79-back cards)

71) AT-ST Driver	6-10	55
72) B-Wing Pilot	5-10	25

Left: Return of the Jedi, Rancor Keeper, Kenner, 1983, $35 MIP.

Right: Return of the Jedi, Teebo, Kenner, 1983, $35 MIP.

73) Han Solo (In Trench Coat) (two coat variations; neither is more rare)

	12-18	40-45
74) Princess Leia Organa (In Combat Poncho)	10-15	55
75) Pruneface	6-10	40
76) Rancor Keeper	5-10	35
77) Teebo	8-10	30-35

78) The Emperor (available carded,
   but originally as a mail-in)

	8-10	20-22(mailer box)
		35-40 (MOC)
79) Wicket W. Warrick	15-20	60

Star Wars: Power of the Force
(Kenner, 1984)

All MOC 1984 figures come with coins and are historically the most demanded in the line.

80) A-Wing Pilot	40-45	125
81) Amanaman	75-90	170

82) Anakin Skywalker (available carded [quite rare],
   but originally as a mail-away offer)

	8-12	
		25-30 (mailer box)
		1,625 (MOC)

83) Artoo-Detoo (R2-D2)

with pop-up light saber	85-95	140
84) Barada	30-40	90
85) EV-9D9	65-75	130
86) Han Solo (In Carbonite Chamber)	75-85	225
87) Imperial Dignitary	40-60	105
88) Imperial Gunner	50-60	110
89) Lando Calrissian (General Pilot)	50-65	95

90) Luke Skywalker (Imperial Stormtrooper Outfit; pure
   white samples are very difficult to acquire)

	75-90	260
91) Luke Skywalker (in Battle Poncho)	55-65	115
92) Lumat	20-25	65
93) Paploo	20-25	60

Left: Power of the Force, Luke Skywalker Jedi Knight Outfit, Kenner, 1984, $165 MIP.

Right: Power of the Force, Romba, Kenner, 1984, $70 MIP.

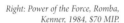

94) Romba	25-35	70
95) Warok	35-40	75
96) Yak Face*	100-120+	1,150

*Yak Face was only released on a Canadian POTF card, or on a European Tri-Logo card without his POTF staff. The character was never available carded or otherwise in the U.S.

Below are e-released POTF figures from earlier SW, ESB, and ROTJ assortments in 1984. Each is carded with a POTF coin sealed on the card front. These figures are rare and in high demand.

AT-AT Driver (POTF w/coin)	5-10	575+
AT-ST Driver (POTF w/coin)	6-10	70+
Biker Scout (POTF w/coin)	10-15	150+
B-Wing Pilot (POTF w/coin)	5-10	65+
Chewbacca (POTF w/coin)	15-20	85+
Darth Vader (POTF w/coin)	15-25	150+
Emperor Palpatine (POTF w/coin)	6-12	110+
Gammorean Guard (POTF w/coin)	5-10	250+
Han Solo (in Trench Coat) (POTF w/coin)	12-18	350+
Jawa (POTF w/coin)	10-12	110+
Leia in Combat Poncho (POTF w/coin)	10-15	75+
Luke Skywalker (Jedi Knight Outfit) (POTF w/coin, green saber)	12-18	165+
Nitko (POTF w/coin; *exceedingly* rare)	5-10	725+
Obi-Wan Kenobi (POTF w/coin)	15-20	135+
C-3PO (See-Threepio; with removable limbs) (POTF w/coin)	5-10	80+
Stormtrooper (POTF w/coin)	8-12	140+
Teebo (POTF w/coin)	8-10	85+
Wicket (POTF w/coin)	15-20	105+
Yoda (POTF w/coin)	15-25	350+

Multi-packed figures

Early Bird Kit (mail-away exclusive run by Kenner: includes Luke, Lei, R2-D2 and Chewbacca)	150-160	425+

Star Wars 12" Figures, Chewbacca, Kenner, 1979, $185 MIP.

Star Wars 12" Figures, Ben (Obi-Wan) Kenobi, Kenner, 1979, $270 MIP.

Star Wars 12" Figures, Jawa, Kenner, 1979, $135 MIP.

Left: Star Wars 12" Figures, Luke Skywalker, Kenner, 1979, $220 MIP.

Right: Star Wars 12" Figures, IG88, Kenner, 1980, $490 MIP.

Star Wars, Carrying Case, Kenner, 1978, $30 MIP.

12" figures

Star Wars

Boba Fett	135	350
C-3PO	30	130
Chewbacca	50	185
Darth Vader	50	185
Han Solo	110	280
Jawa	55	135
Luke Skywalker	70	220
Obi-Wan Kenobi	75	270
Princess Leia Organa	85	220
R2-D2	45	110
Stormtrooper	50	160

Empire Strikes Back

Boba Fett	135	875 (due to
packaging difference: ESB box)		
IG-88	175	490

Carrying cases

Star Wars

24-figure carrying case (commonly missing handle;		
torn plastic)	12-14	25-30

Empire Strikes Back

Darth Vader	8-12	25-30
Mini-Figure	10-12	25-30

Return of the Jedi

C-3PO	10-12	30-35
Darth Vader (with three figures)	8-12	225
Laser Rifle	8-10	30-35

Creatures

Star Wars

Patrol Dewback	20	85

Empire Strikes Back

Hoth Wampa	12-15	32-37
Tauntaun, solid belly	12-15	35-40
Tauntaun, split belly	12-15	45-50

Return of the Jedi

Rancor	30	70-75

Mini-rigs

AST-5	5-6	15
CAP-2	5-8	20
Desert Sail Skiff	10	15
Forest Ranger	5-8	15
INT-4	5-8	15-20
ISP-6	5-8	25
MLC-3	5-8	25
MTV-7	5-8	30
Radar Laser Cannon	5-8	15-20
Tri-Pod Laser Cannon	5-8	15-18
Vehicle Maintenance Energizer	5-8	15-18

Playsets

Star Wars

Cantina Adventure Set (Sears exclusive; with exclusive Blue Snaggletooth)	150	420-450+
Creature Cantina	25	100
Death Star Space Station	75-90	320
Droid Factory	50	135
Land of the Jawas	40	85

Empire Strikes Back

Cloud City Playset (Sears exclusive; with Lobot, Han Solo Bespin Outfit, Dengar, and Ugnaught)	95	300+
Dagobah Playset	22	80
Darth Vader's Star Destroyer	32	115

Hoth Ice Planet	25	80
Imperial Attack Base	20	60
Rebel Command Center (Sears exclusive; with R2-D2 [sensorscope], Luke Hoth and AT-AT Commander)	45	105
Turret and Probot	22	100

Return of the Jedi

Ewok Village	38	80
Jabba the Hutt	17	60
(Salacious Crumb, MISB from above)	5	
Jabba the Hutt Dungeon		
(with Amanaman, Barada, and EV-9D9)	175	250+
Jabba the Hutt Dungeon		
(with 8-D8, Klaatu, and Nitko)	30-35	60+

Vehicles/Accessories

Star Wars

Darth Vader's Tie Fighter	30	125
Imperial Cruiser	20	45
Imperial TIE Fighter	25	100
Imperial Troop Transport	20	65
Jawa Sandcrawler (battery-operated)	220	525+
Land Speeder	10-12	40-45
Millennium Falcon	80	350
Sonic Land Speeder (battery-operated)	180	500
X-Wing Fighter	15-20	80

Empire Strikes Back

AT-AT	85	160
Rebel Transport	35	80
Scout Walker	20-22	40
Slave I (with non-poseable Han Solo in Carbonite)	45-50	125
Snowspeeder	40-45	100
Twin-Pod Cloud Car	35	80

Empire Strikes Back, Darth Vader's Star Destroyer, Kenner, 1980, $115 MIP.

Return of the Jedi

B-Wing Fighter	60	150
Ewok Combat Glider	10	30
Imperial Shuttle	150	500
Speeder Bike	15-20	55-60
TIE Interceptor	40	90
Y-Wing Fighter	55-60	150-160

Power of the Force

Ewok Battle Wagon	75	190
Imperial Sniper Vehicle	35	55
One-Man Sand Skimmer	20	45
Security Scout Vehicle	30+	75+
Tatooine Skiff	175	350-375+

Star Wars: Droids

(Kenner, 1985)

Figures

A-Wing Pilot	40-45	90
Boba Fett	15-25	650+
C-3PO (See-Threepio; not gold-chromed, but solid, multi-colored plastic with painted eyes)	70-75	175
Jann Tosh	18-20	50
Jord Dusat	20	40
Kea Moll	20	40
Kez-Iban	20	40
R2-D2 (Artoo-Deeto; with simplified body markings, yet with same sculpt as regular 1977 R2-D2)	55	125
Sise Fromm	55	250
Thall Joben	20	40
Tig Fromm	50	115
Uncle Gundy	20	30-35

Vehicles

ATL Interceptor	25	65

Empire Strikes Back, Twin Pod Cloud Car, Kenner, 1980, $80 MIP.

A-Wing Fighter	165	360
Imperial Side Gunner	15-20	55

Star Wars: Ewoks
(Kenner, 1985)

Figures

Dulok Scout	15	30
Dulok Shaman	15	30
King Gorneesh	15	30
Logray	12-15	40
Urgah Lady Gorneesh	12-15	30
Wicket	15-20	45

Vehicles and Playsets

Ewoks Fire Cart	5-8	15-20
Ewoks Treehouse	15-20	50
Ewoks Woodland Wagon	5-8	30

Star Wars Episode I: The Phantom Menace
(Hasbro 1998/99-2000)

Figures, 1999

Adi Gallia	3	10
Anakin Skywalker (Naboo)	3	7
Anakin Skywalker (Naboo Pilot)	3	12
Anakin Skywalker (Tatooine)	3	12
Battle Droid (four variations: "star" blaster damage, silver painted lines, light sand marks, dark sand marks)	3	7-9
Boss Nass	3	8
C-3PO	3	8
Captain Panaka	3	8
Captain Tarpals	3	10
Chancellor Valorum	3	10
Darth Maul (Jedi Duel)	3	5
Darth Maul (Sith Lord)	3	12

Left: Episode 1: The Phantom Menace, Darth Sidious, Hasbro, 1999, $12 MIP.

Right: Episode 1: The Phantom Menace, Queen Amidala, Hasbro, 1999, $12 MIP.

Episode 1: The Phantom Menace, Destroyer Droid, Hasbro, 1999, $10 MIP each.

Darth Maul (Tatooine)	3	7
Darth Sidious	3	12
Darth Sidious Holograph	3-5	25
Destroyer Droid	3	10
Gasgano and Pit Droid	3	10
Jar Jar Binks	3	8
Ki-Adi-Mundi	3	10
Mace Windu	3	12
Naboo Royal Guard	3-5	20
Naboo Royal Security	3	7
Nute Gunray	3	6
Obi-Wan Kenobi (Jedi Duel)	3	10
Obi-Wan Kenobi (Jedi Knight)	3	15
Obi-Wan Kenobi (Naboo)	3	7
Ody Mandrell with Otoga 222 Pit Droid	3	7
OOM-9	3	7
Padmé Naberrie	3	10
Queen Amidala (Coruscant)	3	15
Queen Amidala (Naboo)	3	12
Qui-Gon Jinn (Jedi Duel)	3	10
Qui-Gon Jinn (Naboo)	3	7
R2-D2	3	7
Ric Olié	3	8
Rune Haako	3	6
Senator Palpatine	3	12
Watto	3	8
Yoda	3	8

Figures, 2000

Destroyer Droid (Battle Damaged)	3	8
Jar Jar Binks (Naboo Swamp)	3	15
Pit Droids (2 pack)	3-5	20
Queen Amidala (Battle)	3	25+
Qui-Gon Jinn (Jedi Master)	3	15-18

Left: Episode 1: The Phantom Menace, R2-B1 Astromech Droid, Hasbro, 1999, $20 MIP.

Right: Episode 1: The Phantom Menace, TC-14 Protocol Droid, Hasbro, 1999, $30 MIP.

R2-B1	3	20+
Sio Bibble	8-12	35-40
TC-14	3-5	30+

Accessories and accessory sets

Flash Cannon (Electronic)	6-8	10-12
Gungan Energy Ball Catapult Set (Electronic)	6-8	10-12
Hyper-Drive Repair Kit Accessory Set	10-12	20+
Naboo Accessory Set	3	6
Pod Racer Fuel Station Accessory Set	10-12	20+
Rappel Line Attack Accessory Set	10-12	20+
Sith Accessory Set	3	6
Tatooine Accessory Set	3	6
Tatooine Disguise Accessory Set	10-12	20+
Underwater Accessory Set	3	6

Cinema scenes

Mos Espa Encounter	5-8	10-12
Tatooine Showdown	5-8	10-12
Watto's Box	12-14	25

Creatures

Ammo Wagon and Falumpaset	5	25
Battle Bag (Sea Creatures)	3	5-8
Battle Bag (Swamp Creatures)	3	5-8
Eopie with Qui-Gon Jinn	30-35	70+
Fambaa and Gungan Warrior (FAO exclusive)	40-45	100
Jabba Glob	3	5-8
Jabba the Hutt with 2-Headed Announcer	15	30
Kaadu and Jar Jar Binks	2	5
Opee and Qui-Gon Jinn	5	10

Deluxe figures

Darth Maul	3-5	8
Obi-Wan Kenobi	3-5	8
Qui-Gon Jinn	3-5	8

Exclusive figures

Darth Maul Holograph (Wal-Mart exclusive)	6	12
Qui-Gon Jinn Holograph (Wal-Mart exclusive)	6	12

Multi-packs

Darth Maul and Sith Infiltrator	6	12
Final Lightsaber Duel	6	12
Figure Collector 2-Pack	6	12
Commtech 2-Pack	6	12

Playsets and Carry Cases

Comm-Tech Reader	2	4
R2-D2 Carry Case (with Destroyer Droid)	8	20
Theed Generator Complex (with Battle Droid)	8	20
Theed Hangar (with Qui-Gon Jinn)	8	15

Sneak Preview

Mace Windu (mail-away exclusive)	3	6
STAP (with Battle Droid)	6	12

Vehicles

Anakin's Podracer (with Anakin Skywalker)	10	20
Armored Scout Tank (with Battle Droid)	10	25
Droid Fighters	5	12
Flash Speeder	3	8
Gungan Assault Cannon (with Jar Jar Binks)	5	12
Gungan Scout Sub (with Obi-Wan Kenobi)	5	22
Naboo Starfighter	8	20+
Naboo Royal Starship (with red R-2 unit)	65-70	125+
Sebulba's Podracer (with Sebulba)	10	20
Sith Speeder (with Darth Maul)	3	6
Sith Attack Speeder (with Darth Maul)	5-10	20+
Stap (with Battle Droid)	6	12
Trade Federation Tank	8-10	25

12" figures

Anakin Skywalker	5	15

Episode 1: The Phantom Menace 12" Figures, R2-A6 ($15 MIP) and Pit Droids ($20 MIP), Hasbro, 1999.

Anakin Skywalker (with Theed Hangar Droid)	5	15
Aurra Sing (Masterpiece Edition)	5	15-20
Battle Droid	5	20
Battle Droid Commander	5	15
Boss Nass	5	15-20
C-3PO (Electronic)	5	15
Chancellor Valorum and Senate Guard		
(Star Wars Fan Club exclusive)	15-18	30-40
Darth Maul	8-10	25
Darth Maul (Electronic)	5	15
Darth Maul with Sith Speeder	12-15	30
Jar Jar Binks	5	18-22
Jar Jar (Electronic)	5	15
Mace Windu	5	15
Obi-Wan Kenobi	5	20
Pit Droids	5	15-20
Qui-Gon Jinn	5	20
Qui-Gon Jinn (Electronic)	5	15
Qui-Gon Jinn with Poncho	5	15
R2-A6	5	15
Sebulba with Chubas	10	25-30
TC-14 (Kay-Bee exclusive)	5	15
Watto	5	15

Queen Amidala Collection

Beautiful Braids Padmé	5	15
Hidden Majesty Queen Amidala	5	10
Royal Elegance Queen Amidala	5	10
Ultimate Hair Queen Amidala	5	10

Portrait Edition

Black Travel Gown	5	20
Defense of Naboo (Queen Amidala and		
Qui-Gon Jinn; exclusive)	15-20	150+
Red Senate Gown	5	20
Return to Naboo	5	25

Star Wars: Power of the Force II

(Kenner, 1994/95-99)

Note: This is the "new" Star Wars line that provided rabid and clamoring Star Wars collectors with the first new assortment of Star Wars figures in 10 years with their Series One release in late 1994. This first assortment of new figures was snatched off of the pegs, and the toys were met with a small amount of criticism about their highly-masculine proportions—a problem that Hasbro quickly alleviated with the next two waves of figures. The Power of the Force II line was named by Hasbro after the hard-to-find last-run (1984) of figures from the vintage line, with the "II" designation designed by collectors. Regardless, this run of Star Wars action figures was as impressive as their original 1977-84 releases, and provided Hasbro the opportunity to give Star Wars fans new and more accurate sculpts of figures from the original trilogy (Episodes IV-VI), along with never-before created toys based on character designs which were not used in the vintage line. With the additions of characters such as Garindan, Biggs Darklighter, Ishi Tib, Lak Sivrak, and many, many others, the Star Wars toy franchise rose from the ashes and dominated the secondary market once again.

Figures, 1995

Ben (Obi-Wan) Kenobi (short lightsaber)	4	15
Ben (Obi-Wan) Kenobi (long lightsaber)	5	25
Boba Fett	4	20
Boba Fett (circle variation)	50	350
C-3PO	3	10
Chewbacca	3	15
Darth Vader (short lightsaber)	2	15
Darth Vader (long lightsaber)	4	25
Han Solo	3	15
Lando Calrissian	3	10
Luke Skywalker (short lightsaber)	4	15
Luke Skywalker (long lightsaber)	4	25
Luke Skywalker (X-Wing Pilot)	3	15
Princess Leia Organa	3	15-20

Star Wars Power of the Force II, Luke Skywalker in Stormtrooper Disguise, Hasbro, 1996, $15 MIP.

R2-D2	3	15
Stormtrooper	3	12

Figures, 1996

Death Star Gunner	3	20
Greedo	3	20
Han Solo (Carbonite)	3	6-8
Han Solo (Hoth Gear)	3	15
Jawas	3	15
Luke Skywalker (Dagobah Fatigues; short lightsaber)	3	15
Luke Skywalker (long lightsaber)	5	25
Luke Skywalker (Jedi Knight)	3	15
Luke Skywalker (Stormtrooper Disguise)	3	15
Momaw Nadon (Hammerhead)	3	15
R5-D4	3	15
Sandtrooper	3	15
TIE Fighter Pilot	3	6-8
Tusken Raider	3	20
Yoda	3	12

Figures, 1997

Admiral Ackbar	3	10
ASP-7 Droid	3	10
AT-ST Driver	3	12
Bib Fortuna	3	10
Bossk	3	12
Darth Vader (Shadows of the Empire)	4	25-30
Dengar	3	10
Emperor Palpatine	3	10
Emperor's Royal Guard	3	10
EV-9D9	3	12
4-LOM	3	12
Gamorrean Guard	3	10
Garindan	3	7-8
Grand Moff Tarkin	3	20-25

Han Solo (Bespin Gear)	3	7
Han Solo (Endor Gear)	3	12
Hoth Rebel Soldier	3	10
Lando Calrissian (Skiff Guard Disguise)	3	10
Luke Skywalker (Ceremonial Outfit)	3	8
Luke Skywalker (Hoth Gear)	3	10
Malakili (Rancor Keeper)	3	10
Nien Nunb	3	10
Ponda Baba	3	7
Princess Leia Organa (Jabba's Prisoner)	3	15-20
Rebel Fleet Trooper	3	10
Saelt-Marae (Yak Face)	3	12
Snowtrooper	3	8
2-1B Medical Droid	3	10
Weequay	3	7

Figures, 1998

Episode I; Flashback Photos

Ben (Obi-Wan) Kenobi	5	10
Chewbacca (Hoth)	5	10
Darth Vader	5	10
Emperor Palpatine	5	10
Luke Skywalker (Floppy Hat)	3	8
Princess Leia Organa (Ceremonial Gown)		
(Amidala Photo with no make-up)	5	10
(Amidala Photo with make-up)	n/a	1000+
R2-D2 with Launching Lightsaber		
(lightsaber on right side)	5	40+
(lightsaber on left side)	5	10
Yoda with Boiling Pot	5	10

Freeze Frame figures

The following figures sell for the same amounts as their earlier-released MOC counterparts: 8D8, Admiral Ackbar, Ben Kenobi, Darth Vader, Emperor

Palpatine, Emperor's Royal Guard, EV-9D9, Gammorean Guard, Grand Moff Tarkin, Han Solo, Han Solo Bespin Gear, Han Solo Carbonie Block, Han Solo Endor, Hoth Rebel Soldier, Lando Skiff Guard, Luke Sykwalker Ceremonial, Malakili, Princess Leia as Jabba's Prisoner, Princess Leia in Ewok Celebration Gear, Saelt-Marae, and Stormtrooper. The rare and harder-to-find exceptions are listed as follows:

AT-AT Driver (mail-away)	10	20
AT-ST Driver	15-20	60+
Boba Fett	20-25	30-35+
Death Star Droid (mail-away)	10	20
Death Star Trooper (mail-away)	10	20
Hoth Snowtrooper	10	20
Luke Stormtrooper	10	20
Nien Nunb	10	20
Pote Snitkin (mail-away)	10	20
Princess Leia Hoth (mail-away)	10	20
Rebel Fleet Trooper	10	20
Ree-Yees (mail-away)	10	20
Sandtrooper	35-40	125-140
TIE Fighter Pilot	10-12	25
Weequay	120+	350+

Freeze Frame Figures

Re-released previous figures with Freeze Frame Action Slides. Note: These are for U.S. versions only; also, a brief explanation of the slides is appropriate: Freeze Frame Action Slides were used to depict "Actual Movie Scenes" that you could "See and Project" with the mail-away Freeze Frame viewer (i.e. "Luke's Microbinoculars").

Biggs Darklighter	3	15
Captain Piett	5-8	25
Chewbacca (Boushh's Bounty)	3	15
C-3PO with Removable Limbs	3	15
Darth Vader (Removable Helmet)	6-8	30
8-D8	3	10
Endor Rebel Soldier	3	10

Star Wars Power of the Force II, Endor Rebel Soldier, Freeze Frame Figure, Hasbro, $10 MIP.

Power of the Force II, R2-D2 with holographic Leia, Comm Tech Chip Figures, Hasbro, 1999, $30 MIP.

Ewoks: Wicket and Logray	4-5	15
Ishi Tib	3	15
Lak Sivrak	3	15
Lando Calrissian (General's Gear)	3	18
Lobot	3	15-18
Luke Skywalker (Bespin Gear)	3	10
Luke Skywalker (Blastshield Helmet)	3	12
Mon Mothma	3	15
Orrimaarko (Prune Face)	3	15
Princess Leia Organa (all new likeness)	3	10
Princess Leia Organa (Ewok Celebration Outfit)	3	12
R2-D2 with Datalink	3	15
Ugnaughts	3	12
Zuckuss	3	25

Figures, 1999

CommTech Chip figures

Darth Vader with Interrogation Droid	5	12
Greedo (Cantina)	4	10
Han Solo (Cantina)	4	10
Jawa with Gonk Droid	3	8
Luke Skywalker with T-16 Model	3	8
R2-D2 with Holographic Leia	12	30
Stormtrooper	5	15

Episode I Flashback Photos

Anakin Skywalker	3	12
Aunt Beru	3	12
C-3PO (Desert Worn)	3	10

Figures, 2000

CommTech Chip figures

Admiral Motti	5	20
Princess Leia Organa with Sporting Blaster	3	10

Power of the Force II, Millennium Falcon Carrying Case with Scanning Crew figure, Hasbro, 2000, $55 MIP.

Vehicles and Accessories

Carrying Cases

Millennium Falcon Carry Case		
(with Imperial Scanning Crew Trooper)	25	55
Millennium Falcon Carry Case		
(with Wedge Antilles)	12-15	25
Power Of The Force Carry Case	10-12	20
Talking C-3P0 Carry Case	12-15	25

Cinema Scenes

Star Wars

Cantina Aliens	5-8	10-12
Cantina Showdown	5-8	10-12
Death Star Escape	12-15	30+
Purchase of the Droids	5-8	15

Empire Strikes Back

Mynock Hunt	12-15	30-35+

Return Of The Jedi

Final Jedi Duel	10-12	20-25
Jabba's Dancers	4-5	10
Jabba's Skiff Guards	4-5	10
Jedi Spirits	4-5	10
Rebel Pilots	5-6	12

Complete Galaxy

Dagobah with Yoda	7	12-15
Death Star with Darth Vader	7	12-15
Endor with Ewok	12-15	30+
Tatooine with Luke Skywalker	12-15	30+

Creatures

Bantha (with Tusken Raider)	15-20	50-55+
Dewback (with Sandtrooper)	5-6	10

Top: Power of the Force II, Dewback with Sandtrooper, Hasbro, $10 MIP.
Bottom: Power of the Force II, Ronto with Jawa, Hasbro, $10 MIP.

Jabba The Hutt (with Han Solo)	5-6	10
Rancor (with Luke Skywalker)	20-25	50-55+
Ronto (with Jawa)	5-6	10
Tauntan (with Han Solo in Hoth Gear)	25-35	100+
Tauntan (with Luke Skywalker in Hoth Gear)	6-8	12-15
Wampa (with Luke Skywalker in Hoth Gear)	15-20	40+

Deluxe figures

Boba Fett with Firing Missile launcher	5-6	10-12
Han Solo with Smuggler's Flight Pack	5-6	10-12
Hoth Rebel Soldier with Anti-Vehicle Laser Cannon	5-6	10-12
Luke Skywalker with Desert Sport Skiff	5-6	10-12
Probe Droid	5-6	10-12
Snowtrooper with E-Web Heavy Repeating Blaster	5-6	10-12
Stormtrooper (Crowd Control)	5-6	10-12

Electronic F/X

Ben (Obi-Wan) Kenobi	5	10
Darth Vader	5	10
Emperor Palpatine (with Lightning Bolts)	5	10
Luke Skywalker Jedi Knight	5	10
R2-D2	5	10

Gunner Stations

Millennium Falcon w/ Han Solo	5	10
Millennium Falcon w/ Luke Skywalker	5	10
Tie Fighter w/ Darth Vader	10-12	25

Mail-aways

1995 Figures

Han Solo as Stormtrooper (Kellogg's)	4-5	12-15

1997 Figures

Spirit of Obi-Wan (Frito-Lay)	4	6-8
Cantina Band Member (Star Wars Fan Club)	3-5	10-12

Power of the Force II, Kabe and Muftak, Star Wars Fan Club Exclusive, Hasbro, 1998, $12 MIP.

B'omarr Monk (Star Wars Fan Club)	3-5	10-12
Luke Skywalker Jedi Knight (Theater Edition)	5	25-30+

1998 Figures

AT-AT Driver (Star Wars Fan Club exclusive; Freeze Frame)	10-12	20
Darktrooper (Star Wars Fan Club exclusive; Expanded Universe)	10	25
Death Star Droid (Star Wars Fan Club exclusive; Freeze Frame)	10	20
Death Star Trooper (Star Wars Fan Club exclusive; Freeze Frame)	10	20
Kabe and Muftak (Star Wars Fan Club)	5-6	12
Oola and Salacious Crumb (Star Wars Fan Club)	8-10	15-20
Pote Snitkin (Star Wars Fan Club exclusive; Freeze Frame)	10	20
Princess Leia Organa (Hoth Gear) (Star Wars Fan Club exclusive; Freeze Frame)	10	20
Spacetrooper (Star Wars Fan Club exclusive; Expanded Universe)	10-12	25
Ree-Yees (Star Wars Fan Club exclusive; Freeze Frame)	10	20

Accessories

Freeze Frame Slide Holder	5-6	12-15
Freeze Frame Viewer (slide viewer created in the image of "Luke's Microbinoculars" and used to view the "Freeze Frame Action Slides" packaged within figures.)	8-10	25

2000 Figures

Wuher (Star Wars Fan Club exclusive)	10	20

Exclusives and Multi-Packs

Max Rebo Band, Wal-Mart

Barquin D'an and Droopy McCool	10	20

Power of the Force II, Han Solo in Bespin Gear, Millennium Minted Coin Collection, Toy 'R Us Exclusive, Hasbro, $12 MIP.

Joh Yowza and Sy Snootles	10	20
Max Rebo and Doda Bodonawieedo	10	20-22

Millennium Minted Coin Collection, Toys 'R Us

C-3PO	5	12
Chewbacca	5	12
Emperor Palpatine	5	12
Han Solo in Bespin Gear	5	12
Luke Skywalker in Endor Gear	5	12
Princess Leia in Endor Gear	5	12
Snowtrooper	5	12

Multi-packs

Classic Edition 4-pack (Toys 'R Us): Reissue of nearly (but not exactly) the same molds of four "vintage" Star Wars figures, Darth Vader, Chewbacca, Han Solo, and Luke Skywalker)	4-6 ea.	40+
Collector Packs (Sams Club): Three different carded figures packaged together at a (then) discounted price. There were six different sets, and they were theme-based on a particular film from the Original Trilogy)	8-10	25-35

Princess Leia Collection

Bespin Han Solo and Bespin Leia	6	10
Ceremonial Luke and Ceremonial Leia	6	10
R2-D2 and Princess Leia	6	10
Wicket the Ewok and Princess Leia in Ewok Attire	6	10

Playsets

Star Wars

Cantina at Mos Eisley 3-D Display Diorama	7	15
Detention Block Rescue	10-12	20
Death Star Escape	10-12	20
Mos Eisley Cantina	10-12	20
(Star Wars Fan Club mail-away exclusive)	7	15

Power of the Force II, Jabba's Palace playset, Hasbro, $15 MIP.

Power of the Force II, Y-Wing Fighter, Hasbro, $60 MIP.

Empire Strikes Back
Hoth Battle   10-12   20

Return of the Jedi
Endor Attack   10-12   20
Jabba's Palace 3-D Display Diorama
   (with unique Han Solo in Carbonite)   7   15

Vehicles

Star Wars
Darth Vader's Tie Fighter   10-15   25
Landspeeder   4-6   10
Luke Skywalker's X-Wing Fighter, "Red Five"
   (Electronic Power F/X)   20-25   50
Luke Skywalker's T-16 Skyhopper   8-10   20
Millennium Falcon (Electronic)   15-20   60
TIE Fighter   6-8   20
X-Wing Fighter (Electronic)   6-8   25
Y-Wing Fighter (with Y-Wing Pilot)   20-25   60+

Empire Strikes Back
AT-AT Walker (Electronic) (with AT-AT Commander
   and AT-AT Driver)   35-45   120+
AT-ST   20-25   40
Rebel Snowspeeder (Electronic)   10-15   25

Return of the Jedi
A-Wing Fighter (with A-Wing pilot)   10-15   20-22
Power Racing Speeder Bike (with Scout Trooper:
   non-removable)   10   30
Speeder Bike (with Leia in Endor Gear)   5-6   15
Speeder Bike (with Luke in Endor Gear)   5-6   15
Speeder Bike (with Scout Trooper)   5-6   15-20
Tatooine Skiff (with Jedi Knight Luke Skywalker)   20-25   50

Power of the Force II 12" Figures, Han Solo and Luke Skywalker in Stormtrooper Disguise, Kay-Bee Exclusive, Hasbro, $55 MIP.

12" figures

Star Wars

C-3PO	12	20
C-3PO and R2-D2 (Electronic; Toys 'R Us exclusive)	12-15	30
Cantina Band Members (six members were made: Doikk Na'ts with Fizz; Figrin D'an with Kloo Horn; Ickabel with Fanfar; Nalan with Bandfill; Tech with Ommni Box; Tedn with Fanfar)	12-20 ea.	25-28 ea.
Chewbacca	15-20	50
Chewbacca in Chains	15	35
Darth Vader	12	25
Dewback with Sandtrooper	20-22	45-50
Grand Moff Tarkin	12	20
Grand Moff Tarkin and Death Star Gunner (FAO exclusive)	35	60
	12	20
Greedo (JC Penney's exclusive)	12	20-22
Han Solo	12	20
Han Solo and Luke Skywalker in Stormtrooper Disguise (Kay-Bee exclusive)	30	55
Jawa	12	20
Luke Skywalker	12	20
Luke Skywalker in Ceremonial Gear	8-10	12
Luke Skywalker in Stormtrooper Disguise	10	15
Luke Skywalker in X-Wing Pilot Gear	10	15
Luke Skywalker Tatooine; Princess Leia in Boushh Disguise; Han Solo in Bespin Fatigues (Kay-Bee exclusive)	20	35-40
Obi-Wan (Ben) Kenobi	12-15	25
Obi-Wan Kenobi vs. Darth Vader (Electronic; JC Penney's exclusive [and later, Kay-Bee])	10	25-30
Obi-Wan Kenobi with Blastshield Helmet	10	15
Ponda Baba	10	15
Princess Leia Organa	10-15	35
R2-D2	12	15
R5-D4 (Wal-Mart exclusive)	12	15-18

Power of the Force II, Electronic Boba Fett, Kay-Bee Exclusive, Hasbro, $40 MIP.

Power of the Force II, Hoth 4-Pack with Luke Skywalker, Han Solo, Snowtrooper, and AT-AT Driver, JC Penney's Exclusive, Hasbro, $40.

Sandtrooper	12	15
Sandtrooper (Orange) (Diamond exclusive)	12-15	20
Stormtrooper	12	15-20
TIE Fighter Pilot	12	15-20
Tusken Raider w/ Blaster	10	15
Tusken Raider w/ Gaffi Stick	10	15
Wedge Antilles and Biggs Darklighter	15-20	35

Empire Strikes Back

AT-AT Driver	8	20
AT-AT Driver (Service Merchandise exclusive)	10-12	22
Boba Fett	12-15	25
Boba Fett (Electronic; Kay-Bee exclusive)	20	40
Han Solo and Tauntaun	20-22	35+
Han Solo in Hoth Gear	10	15
Hoth 4-Pack (JC Penney's exclusive; includes: Han Hoth, Luke Hoth, Snowtrooper, AT-AT driver)	15-20	40
Lando Calrissian	6-8	10
Luke Skywalker Hoth vs. Wampa	20-22	35+
Luke Skywalker in Bespin fatigues	10	15-20
Luke Skywalker in Hoth Gear	10	15
Princess Leia Organa in Hoth Gear (Service Merchandise exclusive)	10	15
R2-D2 w/ Detachable Utility Arms (Wal-Mart exclusive)	12	15-18
Snowtrooper	10	15-20
Yoda	12-15	22

Return of the Jedi

Admiral Ackbar	6-8	12
Anakin Skywalker (Masterpiece Edition; book store exclusive)	15	25-30
Barquin D'an	6-8	12
Chewbacca in Chains	12-15	25
Darth Vader with Removable Helmet (Electronic)	15-20	30-35

Emperor Palpatine	6-8	12
Emperor Palpatine and Royal Guard		
(Target exclusive)	15-20	35-40
Han Solo Endor	10	15
Han Solo in Carbonite Block (Target exclusive)	10	15
Luke Skywalker in Jedi Gear	12-14	20
Luke Skywalker in Jedi Gear and Bib Fortuna		
(FAO exclusive)	15-20	35-40
Princess Leia (Slave Outfit)	12-15	20
Princess Leia Organa and R2-D2 as Jabba's Prisoners		
(FAO exclusive)	15-18	35-40
Speeder Bike with Scout Trooper	25-30	60-65
Wicket the Ewok (Wal-Mart exclusive)	12-15	25

Star Wars: Expanded Universe
(Hasbro, 1998)

Figures

Dark Empire

Clone Emperor Palpatine	6-8	12-15
Imperial Sentinel	6-8	12-15
Luke Skywalker	10-12	15-18
Princess Leia	10-12	15-18

Dark Forces (video game)

Kyle Katarn	6-8	12-15

Heir to the Empire

Grand Admiral Thrawn	15-18	35+
Mara Jade	12-15	25-30

Vehicles

Airspeeder	5	10
Cloud Car	5	10
Cruise Missile Trooper	3	6
Speeder Bike	3	6

Star Wars: Shadows of the Empire
(Hasbro, 1996)

Figures
Chewbacca (Bounty Hunter Disguise)	4	10
Dash Rendar	5-6	12
Leia (Boushh Disguise)	4	10
Luke Skywalker (Imperial Guard Disguise)	5-6	12
Prince Xizor	4	10

Multi-packs
Boba Fett versus IG-88	6-8	10-12
Prince Xizor versus Darth Vader	6-8	10-12

Vehicles
Boba Fett's Slave I	20-25	50-55
Dash Rendar's Outrider	20-25	35-40
Swoop	4	6-8

Star Wars: Power of the Jedi
(Hasbro, 2000-2002)

Note: These figures are a follow-up to the ultra-successful Star Wars: Power of the Force II (1994/95-2000), and they extended this formidable license. The sculpting is even better than the previous line.

Figures, 2000
Anakin Skywalker (Mechanic)	3	7
Battle Droid (Boomer Damage)	5	10
Battle Droid (Security)	5	10
Ben (Obi-Wan) Kenobi (Jedi Knight)	3	7
Boss Nass (Gungan Sacred Place)	3	7
Chewbacca (Dejarik Champion)	3	7
Coruscant Guard	3-5	12
Darth Maul (Final Duel)	3	7
Darth Vader (Dagobah)	3	7
Fode and Beed (Pod Race Announcers)	8	12

Power of the Jedi, Scout Trooper (dirty highlights on left $15 MIP, clean on right $12 MIP), Hasbro, 2000.

Left: Power of the Jedi, Luke Skywalker X-Wing Pilot, Hasbro, 2000, $12 MIP.
Right: Power of the Jedi, Jek Porkins X-Wing Pilot, Hasbro, 2000, $15 MIP.

Gungan Warrior	4	8
Han Solo (Bespin Capture)	3	7
IG-88 (Bounty Hunter)	5-6	15
Jek Porkins (X-Wing Pilot)	5-6	15
K-3PO (Echo Base Protocol Droid)	6	20
Leia Organa (General)	3	7
Mas Amedda	3	7
Mon Calamari (Officer)	3	7
Obi-Wan Kenobi (Jedi)	3	7
Plo Koon (Jedi Master)	4	10
Qui-Gon Jinn (Mos Espa Disguise)	3	7
R2-D2 (Naboo Escape)	4	10
Scout Trooper (Imperial Patrol, clean)	5	12-15
Scout Trooper (dirty highlights)	5	12
Sebulba (Boonta Eve Challenge)	3	7
Tusken Raider (Desert Sniper)	3	7

Figures, 2001

Aurra Sing (Bounty Hunter)	3	7
Bespin Guard (Cloud City Security)	3	7
Chewbacca (Millennium Falcon Mechanic)	3	7
Darth Maul (Sith Apprentice)	3	7
Darth Vader (Emperor's Wrath)	5-6	12
Eeth Koth (Jedi Master)	4	8
Ellorrs Madak (Fan's Choice FIgure No. 1)	6-8	12-15
FX-7 (Medical Droid)	3	7
Han Solo (Death Star Escape)	3	7
Imperial Officer	4	8
Jar Jar Binks (Tatooine)	3	7
Ketwol	3	7
Lando Calrissian (Bespin Escape)	3	7
Leia Organa (Bespin Escape)	3	7
Luke Skywalker (X-Wing Pilot)	5	12
Obi-Wan Kenobi (Cold Weather Gear)	5-6	12
Obi-Wan Kenobi (Jedi Training Gear)	4	8

Power of the Jedi, Queen Amidala Theed Invasion, Hasbro, 2000, $8 MIP.

Power of the Jedi, 25th Anniversary two-packs. Left to right: Obi-Wan Kenobi and Darth Vader Final Duel, Luke Skywalker and Princess Leia Swing to Freedom, Han Solo and Chewbacca Death Star Escape, Hasbro, 2002, $22 MIP each.

Power of the Jedi, Boba Fett 300th Figure Special Edition, Hasbro, 2002, $25 MIP.

Power of the Jedi, Darth Maul & Darth Vader Masters of the Dark Side, Hasbro, 2002, $35 MIP.

Power of the Jedi, Carbon Freezing Chamber playset, Hasbro, 2002, $45 MIP.

"Invasion of Theed" adventure game)	5-8	20-25
		(MISB with game)

Star Tours
(Disney exclusive droids)

Figures

G2-4T	4-5	10-12
RX-24 (Captain REX)	4-5	10-12
R3-D3	4-5	10-12
DL-X2	4-5	10-12
R4-M9	4-5	10-12
WEG-1618	4-5	10-12
G2-9T	4-5	10-12
R5-D2	4-5	10-12
SK-Z38	4-5	10-12
3T-RNE	4-5	10-12
G3-5LE	4-5	10-12
MSE-1T	4-5	10-12

Multi-packs

Darth Vader and Darth Maul:		
Masters Of The Dark Side	10-12	30-35+

Playsets

Carbon-Freezing Chamber playset		
(Star Wars Fan Club exclusive)	20-25	40-45+

Vehicles

Parade Vehicle	8-10	15-20
Starspeeder 3000	10-12	20-25
B-Wing Fighter (with Unique Sullustan Pilot;		
Target exclusive)	25-30	55-60+
Imperial AT-ST and Speeder Bike		
(with Ewok Paploo)	25-30	50-55

Power of the Jedi, Imperial AT-ST and Speeder Bike with Ewok Paploo, Hasbro, 2002, $55 MIP.

Power of the Jedi, Tie Interceptor, Hasbro, 2002, $70 MIP.

Luke Skywalker's Snowspeeder		
(with Dack Ralter)	25-30	60-65+
TIE Bomber (with Imperial Pilot)	25-30	45-50+
TIE Interceptor (with Imperial Pilot)	35-40	65-70+

Star Wars: Saga Collection
(Hasbro, 2002-04)

Note: The Star Wars Saga Collection highlighted the new characters introduced in *Star Wars: Episode II: Attack of the Clones* and added new editions from the Original Trilogy and *Star Wars: Episode I: The Phantom Menace*. This gave Hasbro the opportunity to treat new fans who just came on board with the new trilogy, and appease die-hard Star Wars aficionados with new sculpts of old favorites. Needless to say, the line was met with rousing success. What really made this line collector-friendly was the fact that Hasbro began numbering each new figure release throughout the year, and further, based later releases around a particular theme. Whether the adventures of these figures took place on the frozen tundra of Ice Planet Hoth, the vast and empty wastes of Tatooine, or the decadent society of Jabba's Palace—these stand as some of the finest action figures ever produced.

Figures, 2002

Note: The earliest releases of #'s 1-16 came packaged with light background inserts behind the packaged figures. These background insert variations add $1-2 per MOC (only) figures.

2002-01: Anakin Skywalker		
(Outland Peasant Disguise)	3	6
2002-02: Padmé Amidala (Arena Escape)	3	6
2002-03: Obi-Wan Kenobi (Coruscant Chase)	3	6
2002-04: C-3PO (Protocol Droid)	3	6
2002-05: Kit Fisto (Jedi Master)	4	8
2002-06: Super Battle Droid	4	7
2002-07: Boba Fett (Kamino Escape)	5	10
2002-08: Tusken Raider (Female with child)	3	6
2002-09: Captain Typho (Padmé's Head of Security)	3	6
2002-10: Shaak Ti (Jedi Master)	3	6
2002-11: Battle Droid (Arena Battle)	4	8

Left: *Star Wars: Saga Collection, Boba Fett, Hasbro, 2002, $10 MIP.*

Right: *Star Wars: Saga Collection, Shaak Ti, Hasbro, 2002, $6 MIP.*

Star Wars: Return of the Jedi, Emperor's Royal Guard, Kenner, 1983, $12 MIP.

2002-12: Plo Koon (Arena Battle)	4	8
2002-13: Jango Fett (Kamino Escape)	5	10
2002-14: R2-D2 (Coruscant Sentry)	4	8
2002-15: Geonosian Warrior	3	6
2002-16: Dexter Jettster (Coruscant Informant)	3	6
2002-17: Clone Trooper	5	10
2002-18: Zam Wesell (Bounty Hunter)	2	5
2002-19: Royal Guard (Coruscant Security)	6	12
2002-20: Saesee Tiin (Jedi Master)	4	8
2002-21: Nikto (Jedi Knight)	3	6
2002-22: Anakin Skywalker (Hanger Duel)	3	6
2002-23: Yoda (Jedi Master)	4	8
2002-24: Jar Jar Binks (Gungan Senator)	3	6
2002-25: Taun We (Kamino Cloner)	3	6
2002-26: Luminara Unduli (Jedi Master)	4	8
2002-27: Count Dooku (Dark Lord)	3	6
2002-28: Mace Windu (Geonosian Rescue)	3	6
2002-29: Luke Skywalker (Bespin Duel)	6-8	12-15
("bloody stump" variation)	6-8	20-25
2002-30: Darth Vader (Bespin Duel)	6-8	12-15
2002-31: Jango Fett (Final Battle)	4	8
2002-32: Qui-Gon Jinn (Naboo Battle)	3	6
2002-33: Endor Soldier	3	6
2002-34: Massif (With Geonosian Warrior)	3	6
2002-35: Orn Free Taa (Senator)	3	6
2002-36: Obi-Wan Kenobi (Jedi Starfighter Pilot)	3	6
2002-37: Han Solo (Endor Bunker)	3	6
2002-38: Chewbacca (Cloud City Capture)	3	6
2002-39: Supreme Chancellor Palpatine	3	6
2002-40: Djas Puhr (Alien Bounty Hunter)	3	6
2002-41: Padmé Amidala (Coruscant Attack)	3	6
2002-42: Darth Maul (Sith Training)	3	6
2002-43: Anakin Skywalker (Tatooine Attack)	3	6

Star Wars: Saga Collection, Clone Trooper (Republic Gunship Pilot), Hasbro, 2002, $12 MIP.

Nexu with Snapping Jaw and Attack Roar	5	10
Obi-Wan Kenobi (Kamino Showdown)	5	10
Obi-Wan Kenobi with Force-Flipping Attack	5	10
Spider Droid with Rotating Turret and Firing Cannon	5	10
Super Battle Droid Builder with		
Droid Factory Assembly Mold	5	10
Yoda with Force Powers	5	10

Exclusives

2002

R2-D2 (Toys 'R Us Silver Promotion)	5-10	15
Holiday Edition (R2-D2 and C-3PO)		
(Wal-Mart Christmas)	10	20

2003

Boba Fett (Star Wars Fan Club; Silver Promotion)	5-10	25
Holiday Edition Yoda (Star Wars Fan Club)	5-10	25

2004

Clone Trooper (Toys 'R Us; Silver Promotion)	5-10	15

Hall of Fame

Note: These figures were previously released in the Star Wars Saga line on Star Wars Saga-type cards.

Anakin Skywalker (Geonosis Hangar Duel)	5	10
C-3PO (Death Star Rescue)	5	10
Chewbacca (Escape From Hoth)	5	10
Darth Maul (Theed Hangar Duel)	5	10
Darth Vader (Death Star Clash)	5	10
Han Solo (Flight to Alderaan)	5	10
Luke Skywalker (Tatooine Encounter)	5	10
Obi-Wan Kenobi (Coruscant Chase)	5	10
Princess Leia Organa (Death Star Captive)	5	10
R2-D2 (Tatooine Mission)	5	10

Stormtrooper (Death Star Chase)	5	10
Yoda (Battle of Geonosis)	5	10
Multi-packs		
Battle of Hoth (Toys 'R Us exclusive)	5-8	20-25
Imperial Forces (Toys 'R Us exclusive)	5-8	20-25
Jedi Warriors (Toys 'R Us exclusive)	5-8	20-25
Light Saber Action Pack	5-8	15
Skirmish at Carkoon (Toys 'R Us exclusive)	4	10-15
Ultimate Bounty (Toys 'R Us exclusive)	5-8	20-25

Troop Builder Sets *(Star Wars Fan Club Exclusives)*

Endor Soldiers Troop Builder Set	12	20-25
Rebel Trooper Builder Set	12	20-25
Sandtroopers Troop Builder Set	12	20-25
Stormtroopers Troop Builder Set	12	20-25

Playsets

Geonosis Battle Arena	15-20	30-35

Screen Scenes

Attack of the Clones

Geonosian War Room (Poggle the Lesser, San Hill, Count Dooku)	10	15
Geonosian War Room (Nute Gunray, Shu Mai, Passel Argente)	10	15
Jedi Council (Mace Windu, Even Piell, Oppo Rancisis)	10	15

Star Wars: Saga Collection, Jango Fett's Slave 1, Hasbro, $20 MIP.

Phantom Menace, The
Jedi Council (Yarael Poof, Depa Billaba, Yaddle)   10   15

Star Wars
Death Star Trash Compactor
(Luke Skywalker and Han Solo)   5-8   20
Death Star Trash Compactor
(Princess Leia and Chewbacca)   5-8   20

Vehicles

Attack of the Clones
Anakin Skywalker's Speeder   6   10-12
Anakin Skywalker's Swoop Bike   6   10
Darth Tyranus's Geonosian Speeder Bike   6   12
Obi-Wan Kenobi's Jedi Starfighter   6-8   15
Obi-Wan Kenobi's Jedi Starfighter
(with Obi-Wan Kenobi; Kay-Bee exclusive)   6-8   20
Republic Gunship   10-12   25-30
Jango Fett's Slave I   10-12   20
Zam Wesell's Speeder   6   12

Classic Trilogy
A-Wing Fighter (with Pilot)   10-12   20
Imperial Shuttle (FAO exclusive)   60-65   120+
Luke Skywalker and Landspeeder   12-15   20-25
Luke Skywalker's X-Wing Fighter   12-15   20-25
Red Leader's X-Wing Fighter (Death Star Trench)   15-20   40
TIE Bomber   15-20   40
TIE Fighter (Imperial Dogfight)   10-12   20

Ultra figures

Classic Trilogy
C-3PO (Tatooine Encounter)   6-8   10-12
Ewok with Attack Glider (Assault on Endor)   8-10   20

Star Wars: Saga Collection 12" Figures, Clone Trooper (red highlights) and Clone Trooper Commander (yellow highlights), Kay-Bee Exclusives, Hasbro, $30 MIP each.

32518

Ki-Adi-Mundi™

MADE IN CHINA

Star Wars: Saga Collection 12" Figures, Ki-Adi-Mundi, Star Wars Fan Club,
Hasbro, $25 MIP.

General Rieekan (Hoth Evacuation)	6-8	15
Jabba's Palace Court Denizens	6	12
Jabba the Hutt (Jabba's Palace)	6	12
Wampa (Hoth Attack)	6	12

Prequel Trilogy

Jango Fett (Kamino Confrontation)	4	10
Obi-Wan Kenobi (Kamino Confrontation)	5	12

12" figures

Attack of the Clones

Anakin Skywalker	12	25
Anakin Skywalker (Slashing Lightsaber Action)	10	20
Clone Commander	10	22
Clone Trooper (black and white)	10	22
(red highlights, Kay-Bee)	12-15	30
(yellow highlights, Kay-Bee)	12-15	30
Clone Trooper (Captain)	10	22
Count Dooku	10	25
Geonosian Warrior	10	20
Jango Fett, Collector's exclusive	12-15	30
Jango Fett (Electronic Battling)	8	15
Ki-Adi-Mundi (Jedi Council, Star Wars Fan Club)	10-12	20-25
Mace Windu (Jedi Council)	10	25
Obi-Wan Kenobi (Attack of the Clones)	10	25
Obi-Wan Kenobi (Electronic Battling)	10	20
Padmé Amidala	8	15
Plo Koon (Jedi Council, Star Wars Fan Club)	50-55	100+
Super Battle Droid	10	20
Yoda (with hoverchair and accessories)	12	25-30
Zam Wesell	6	10

Star Wars

Ben (Obi-Wan) Kenobi (new face sculpt)	10	20
Garindan	12	25

Star Wars: Saga Collection 12" Figures, Imperial Officer, Hasbro, $12 MIP.

Star Wars: Saga Collection 12" Figures, Luke Skywalker & Tauntaun, Toys 'R Us Exclusive, Hasbro, $55 MIP.

Star Wars: Saga Collection 12" Figures, Gamorrean Guard, Kay-Bee Exclusive, Hasbro, $35 MIP.

Star Wars: Clone War Saga, Anakin Skywalker, Mace Windu, Obi-Wan Kenobi, Asajj Ventress, Hasbro, 2003, $10 MIP each.

Han Solo	10	20
Jawa 2-pack	12-15	30

Empire Strikes Back, The
Dengar	10	25
Imperial Officer	6-8	10-12
Luke Skywalker and Tauntaun (Toys 'R Us)	15-20	55
Zuckuss	10	25

Return Of The Jedi
AT-ST Driver	12-15	30
Biker Scout	15-20	40+
Ewok 2-pack (Logray and Keoulkeech)	12-15	35
Gamorrean Guard (Kay-Bee exclusive)	8	15-20
Lando Calrissian (Skiff Disguise)	8-10	20
Luke Skywalker, Jedi Knight (Slashing Lightsaber Action)	8	15
Princess Leia (Boushh Disguise) with Han Solo Carbonite Block	12-15	40
Princess Leia with Speeder Bike (Target exclusive)	18-20	50

Star Wars: Clone Wars Saga
(Hasbro, 2003)

From the "Clone Wars" Cartoon Network animated series. For the non-animated figures, see Star Wars Saga figures, 2003.

Series 1
Anakin Skywalker	5	10
Asajj Ventress	5	10
Mace Windu	5	10
Obi-Wan Kenobi	5	10

Series 2
Clone Trooper (red, blue, yellow)	5	10
Count Dooku	5	10
Durge	5	10-12
Yoda	5	10

Star Wars: Original Trilogy Collection, Luke Skywalker (Dagobah Training handstand), Hasbro, 2004, $20 MIP.

Series 3

ARC Trooper	5	10
Anakin Skywalker (Battle Damage)	5-7	12
Clone Trooper Captain	5	12
Clone Trooper Commander	5	12
Clone Trooper Lieutenant	5	12
General Grievous	5	10

Deluxe figures

Clone Trooper with Speeder Bike	5	10-12
Durge with Swoop	5	12-15
Spider Droid	5	10

Multi-packs; non-animated

Anakin and Clone Lieutenant (value-pack)	5	12
ARC Trooper and Clone Trooper (value-pack)	5	12
Clone Trooper Army (Set of 3: blue, green, or white)	8	12-15
Clone Trooper Army (Set of 3- red or yellow)	10-12	20-25
Destroyer Droid Battle Launcher	5	10
Droid Army (3-pack)	5	10-12
Jedi Knight Army (3-pack)	5	10-12
Yoda and Clone Commander (value-pack)	5	12

Vehicles

Anakin Skywalker's Jedi Starfighter	10-12	20
Armored Assault Tank (AAT)	10-12	20
Command Gunship	12-15	30
Geonosian Starfighter	10	20
Hailfire Droid	10	20
Jedi Starfighter	10	20

Star Wars: Original Trilogy Collection

(Hasbro, 2004)

Figures, 2004

OTC-01: Luke Skywalker (Dagobah Training) (handstand)	5	20

Star Wars: Original Trilogy Collection, Cloud Car Pilot, Hasbro, 2004, $8 MIP.

OTC-01: Luke Skywalker (Dagobah Training) (standing up)	5	10
OTC-02: Yoda (Dagobah Training)	3	8
OTC-03: Spirit Obi-Wan (Dagobah Training)	3	8
OTC-04: R2-D2 (Dagobah Training)	3	8
OTC-05: Luke Skywalker (X-Wing Pilot)	3	8
OTC-06: Luke Skywalker (Jedi Knight)	3	8
OTC-07: Han Solo	3	8
OTC-08: Chewbacca	3	8
OTC-09: Princess Leia	3	8
OTC-10: Darth Vader (Throne Room)	3	8
OTC-11: Scout Trooper	3	8
OTC-12: R2-D2	3	8
OTC-13: C-3PO	3	8
OTC-14: Boba Fett	5	10-12
OTC-15: Obi-Wan Kenobi	3	8
OTC-16: Stormtrooper	3	8
OTC-17: Wicket	3	8
OTC-18: Princess Leia (Cloud City)	3	8
OTC-19: Cloud Car Pilot	3	8
OTC-20: Lobot (Cloud City)	5	10-12
OTC-21: TIE Fighter Pilot	3	8
OTC-22: Greedo	3	10
OTC-23: Tusken Raider	3	10
OTC-24: Jawas	3	10
OTC-25: Snowtrooper	3	8
OTC-26: Luke Skywalker (Bespin Gear)	3	10
OTC-27: IG-88	3	10
OTC-28: Bossk	3	10
OTC-29: Darth Vader (Hoth)	3	10
OTC-30: Gamorrean Guard	3	8
OTC-31: Bib Fortuna	3	8
OTC-32: Lando Calrissian (Skiff Guard)	3	8

OTC-33: Princess Leia (Sail Barge)	3	8
OTC-34: Darth Vader (Death Star)	3	8
OTC-35: Han Solo (AT-ST Driver)	5	12-14
OTC-36: General Madine	5	12-14
OTC-37: Lando Calrissian (General)	5	12-14
OTC-38: Imperial Trooper	5	15-20

Figures, 2005

Wave 1: Coruscant

2005-01: Pablo-Jill (Geonosis Arena)	5	10-12
2005-02: Yarua (Coruscant Senate)	5	10-12
2005-03: Sly Moore (Coruscant Senate)	5	10-12

Wave 2: Naboo

2005-04: Queen Amidala (Celebration Ceremony)	5	10-12
2005-05: Rabé (Queen's Chambers)	5	10-12

Wave 3: Cantina

2005-06: Feltipern Trevagg (Cantina)	5	10-12
2005-07: Myo (Cantina)	5	10-12
2005-08: Dannik Jerriko (Cantina Encounter)	5	10-12

Repacks

2005-09: Luke Skywalker (Dagobah Training)	3-4	8
2005-10: Darth Vader (Death Star Hangar)	3-4	8
2005-11: Stormtrooper (Death Star Attack)	3-4	8
2005-12: Sandtrooper (Tatooine Search)	3-4	8
2005-13: Scout Trooper (Endor Raid)	3-4	8
2005-14: Han Solo (Mos Eisley Escape)	3-4	8
2005-15: Chewbacca (Hoth Escape)	3-4	8
2005-16: Yoda (Dagobah Training)	3-4	8

Carry Case

C-3PO carry case (Wal-Mart exclusive)	5-6	15
Darth Vader carry case (Wal-Mart exclusive)	5-6	15

Cinema Scenes

Attack of the Clones

Jedi Council IV (Shaak Ti, Agen Kolar, Stass Allie)	6-8	20

Phantom Menace, The

Jedi Council I (Yoda, Qui-Gon Jinn, Ki-Adi-Mundi)	6-8	20
Jedi Council II (Plo Koon, Obi-Wan, Eeth Koth)	6-8	20
Jedi Council III (Anakin Skywalker, Saesee Tiin, Adi Gallia)	6-8	20

Star Wars (K-Mart exclsuives)

Mos Eisley Cantina I (Dr. Evazan, Wuher, Kitik Keed'kak)	6-8	20
Mos Eisley Cantina II (Obi-Wan Kenobi, Ponda Baba, Zutton)	6-8	20

Exclusives

2004

Darth Vader (Silver Anniversary; Toys 'R Us)	5-6	20
Emperor Palpatine (Executor Transmission; Star Wars Fan Club)	6-8	20
Jawas Holiday Set (2004 Holiday Edition)	6-8	20
Scout Trooper (Star Wars: Battlefront video game)	6	20

2005

Holiday Darth Vader (Star Wars Fan Club)	6-8	20-25
Wedge Antilles (Internet vendors)	6-8	15

Multi-packs

Bounty Hunters - The Hunt for the Millennium Falcon (Diamond exclusive)	30-35
Clone Trooper Troop Builder 4-Pack (Entertainment Earth exclusive)	30-35
Endor Ambush (Toys 'R Us exclusive)	20
Naboo Final Conflict (Toys 'R Us exclusive)	20

Vehicles

Darth Vader's TIE Fighter (with Darth Vader)	12-15	20-25
Millennium Falcon (Electronic Lights and Sounds)	10-15	30
Millennium Falcon Crew (Sam's Club exclusive)	8	15
TIE Fighter	6	15
TIE Fighter and X-Wing Fighter (Costco exclusive 2-Pack)	12	25
Sandcrawler (Diamond exclusive)	20	45
Slave I (with Boba Fett)	10	20
X-Wing Fighter	6	15
Y-Wing Fighter (with Rebel Alliance Pilot)	10-12	25

12" "Vintage" Figures

Boba Fett	12-15	25-30
Chewbacca (Kak-Bee)	10	15-20
Luke Skywalker	10	20
Stormtrooper	10-12	20-25

"Vintage" Figures

Empire Strikes Back, The

Darth Vader	5	10
C-3PO	5	10
Lando Calrissian	3	8
Yoda	5	10

Return of the Jedi

Boba Fett	6-8	12-15
Chewbacca	6-8	12-15
R2-D2	6-8	12-15
Stormtrooper	5	10

Star Wars

Han Solo	5	10
Luke Skywalker	5	10
Obi-Wan Kenobi	5	10
Princess Leia	5	10

Left: Episode III: Revenge of the Sith, Obi-Wan Kenobi (Slashing Attack), Hasbro, 2005, $8 MIP.

Right: Episode III: Revenge of the Sith, Anakin Skywalker (Lightsaber Attack), Hasbro, 2005, $8 MIP.

Left: Episode III: Revenge of the Sith, General Grievous (Four Lightsaber Attack), Hasbro, 2005, $10 MIP.

Right: Episode III: Revenge of the Sith, AT-TE Tank Gunner (Clone Army), Hasbro, 2005, $10 MIP.

Star Wars: Episode III: Revenge of the Sith
(Hasbro, 2005-present)

Figures

#01 Obi-Wan Kenobi (Slashing Attack)	3	8
#02 Anakin Skywalker (Lightsaber Attack)	3	8
#03 Yoda (Firing Cannon)	3	8
#04 Super Battle Droid (Firing Arm Action)	3	8
#05 Chewbacca (Wookie Rage)	3	8
#06 Clone Trooper (Quick Draw Action)	3	10
#07 R2-D2 (Droid Attack)	3	8
#08 General Grevious' Bodyguard (Battle Attack)	3	8
#09 General Grevious (Four Lightsaber Attack)	3	10
#10 Mace Windu (Force Combat)	3	8
#11 Darth Vader (Lightsaber Attack)	3	8
#12 Darth Sidious	3	8
#13 Count Dooku (Sith Lord)	3	8
#14 Chancellor Palpatine (Supreme Chancellor)	3	8
#15 Bail Organa (Republic Senator)	3	8
#16 Plo Koon (Jedi Master)	3	8
#17 Battle Droid (Separatist Army)	3	8
#18 C-3PO (Protocol Droid)	3	8
#19 Padmé (Republic Senator)	3	8
#20 Agen Kolar (Jedi Master)	3	8
#21 Shaak Ti (Jedi Master)	3	8
#22 Kit Fisto (Jedi Master)	3	8
#23 Royal Guard (Senate Security) - Blue	5	12
#23 Royal Guard (Senate Security) - Red	5	12
#24 Mon Mothma (Republic Senator)	3	5
#25 Tarfful (Firing Bowcaster)	3	8
#26 Yoda (Spining Attack)	3	8
#27 Obi-Wan Kenobi (Jedi Kick)	3	8
#28 Anakin Skywalker (Slashing Attack)	3	8

#29 Ki-Adi-Mundi (Jedi Master)	3	8
#30 Saesee Tiin (Jedi Master)	3	8
#31 Luminara Unduli (Jedi Master)	3	8
#32 Aayla Secura (Jedi Knight)	3	8
#33 Clone Commander (Battle Gear)	5	10
#34 Clone Pilot (Firing Cannon)	5	10
#35 Palpatine (Lightsaber Attack)	3	8
#36 General Grievous (Exploding Body)	3	8
#37 Vader's Medical Droid (Chopper Droid)	4	8-10
#38 AT-TE Tank Gunner (Clone Army)	5	10
#39 Polis Massan (Medic)	3	8
#40 Mas Amedda (Republic Senator)	3	8
#41 Clone Trooper (Super-Articulated)	4	8-10
#42 Neimoidian Warrior	3	8
#43 Wookie Warrior	5	10
#44 Destroyer Droid	3	8
#45 Tarkin	5	10
#46 Ask Aak	5	10
#47 Meena Tillis	3	8
#48 R2-D2	3	8
#49 Commander Baccarra	5	10
#50 Anakin Skywalker on Mustafar	3	8
#51 Captain Antilles	3	8
#52 Jett Jukassa	3	8
#53 Utapauan Warrior	3	8
#54 Turbo Tank Driver	5	10
#55 Mustafar Sentry	5	8-10
#56 Obi-Wan Kenobi (Red Leader)	3	8
#57 Commander Gree	5	10
#58 Wookiee Commando	5	10
#59 Commander Bly	5	10
#60 Grievous' Bodyguard	5	10
#61 Passel Argente	3	8

#62 Cat Miin (Shu Mai's Aide)	3	8
#63 Neimoidian Commander	3	8
#64 R4-P17 (Astromech Droid)	5	10-12
#65 Tactical Ops Trooper (Blue Markings)	6-8	12-15
#66 Plo Koon (Hologram)	6-8	12-15
#67 Aayla Secura (Hologram)	6-8	12-15
#68 Wookiee Heavy Gunner	5	10

Battle arena 2-packs

Bodyguard Vs. Obi-Wan (Utapau Landing Platform)	6-8	15-20
Dooku Vs. Anakin (Trade Federation Cruiser)	6-8	15-20
Sidious Vs. Mace (Chancellor's Office)	6-8	15-20

Battle packs

Assault on Hoth (General Veers, Probot, 3 Snowtroopers)	10-12	20-25
Clone Attack on Coruscant (Clone Commander, 4 Clone Troopers)	10-12	20-25
Imperial Throne Room (Emperor, 2 Guards, Stormtrooper, Dignitary)	10-12	20-25
Jedi Temple Assault (Anakin, Clone Pilot, 3 Special Ops Troopers)	10-12	20-25
Jedi Vs. Sith (Anakin, Obi-Wan, Yoda, Asajj, Grievous)	8-10	20
Jedi Vs. Separatists (Anakin, Obi-Wan, Mace, Maul, Jango)	8-10	20
Rebel Vs. Empire (Chewie, Han, Luke, Vader, Stormtrooper)	8-10	20

Creatures

Boga (with Obi-Wan Kenobi)	15-20	35+

Deluxe figures

500th Edition Darth Vader	6-8	12-15
Anakin Skywalker (Changes to Darth Vader)	8-10	20-25
Chancellor Palpatine/Darth Sidious (Transformation)	6-8	10-12

Episode III: Revenge of the Sith, Clone Troopers 3-pack assorted colors, Hasbro, 2005, $15 MIP.

Clone Trooper (Firing Jet Backpack)	6-8	10-12
Clone Troopers (3-pack, assorted colors)	8	12-15+
Crab Droid (with Moving Legs and Missile Launcher)	5	10
Darth Vader (Rebuild Darth Vader)	6-8	12-15
General Grievous (with Secret Lightsaber Attack)	5	10
Obi-Wan Kenobi (with Force Jump Attack)	5	10
Spider Droid (with Firing "Laser" Action)	5	10
Stass Allie with BARC Speeder (with "Exploding" Action)	5	10
Vulture Droid	5	10
Yoda	6-8	12

Evolutions; I-III

Anakin Skywalker to Darth Vader: Anakin Skywalker, Anakin Skyawlker, Darth Vader	12	20
Clone Trooper to Stormtrooper: Clone Trooper, Clone Trooper, Sandtrooper	12	30
Clone Trooper to Sandtrooper: Clone Trooper, Clone Trooper, Sandtrooper	12	25
The Sith: Darth Maul, Count Dooku, Emperor Palpatine	8	18-20

Exclusives

Kay-Bee

Collector's Multi-Pack (nine figures + Silver Darth Vader)	10-12	25-30

Target

Clone Trooper (new markings)	6-8	20+
Darth Vader (Lava Reflection)	15	45-50
Darth Vader (Duel at Mustafar)	6	10-15+
Obi-Wan Kenobi (Duel at Mustafar)	6	10-15+
Utapau Shadow Trooper	8-10	20-25

Toys 'R Us

Holographic Yoda (Kashyyyk Transmission)	6	15-20
Holographic Emperor Palpatine	6	15

Star Wars Shop.com
Covert Ops Clone Trooper   12   25-30

Wal-Mart
Commemorative Episode III DVD
    Collection 1 - Jedi Knights   12   25
Commemorative Episode III DVD
    Collection 2 - Sith Lords   12   25
Commemorative Episode III DVD
    Collection 3 - Clone Troopers   12   25

Playsets
Mustafar Final Duel (includes
    Obi-Wan Kenobi and Darth Vader)   15   35-40
Mustafar Final Duel (includes 4 Bonus Figures;
    Sam's Club exclusive)   15   35-40

Sneak Preview figures
(1 of 4): General Grievous   5   10
(2 of 4): Tion Medon   5   10
(3 of 4): Wookiee Warrior   5   10
(4 of 4): R4-G9   5   10

Sneak Preview vehicles
Anakin's Starfighter   10   20

Vehicles
Anakin's Jedi Starfighter (with Anakin Skywalker;
    Toys 'R Us exclusive)   8   15
ARC-170 Starfighter   10-12   30
AT-RT (with AT-RT Driver)   5   10-12
Barc Speeder (with Barc Trooper)   5   10-12
Droid Tri-Fighter   5   10
Obi-Wan's Jedi Starfighter   10   20
Obi-Wan's Jedi Starfighter (with Obi-Wan Kenobi;
    Toys 'R Us exclusive)   12-15   35

Grievous' Wheel Bike (with General Grievous)	8	15
Plo Koon's Jedi Starfighter	12-15	40
Republic Gunship	10-12	30-35
Wookiee Flyer (with Wookiee Warrior)	6	12

12" figures

Anakin Skywalker/Darth Vader (Ultimate Villain)	12-15	40-45+
Barriss Offee	8	15-20
Chewbacca (Kay-Bee Toys exclusive)	8	15-20
Clone Trooper	8	20
Darth Sidious	8	20
General Grievous	12-15	30
Shaak Ti	8	15-20

Strawberry Shortcake
(Kenner, 1979-85)

Series 1

Note: With first Issue dolls some of these early releases came without a pet and with more points of articulation than their second issue releases.

Apple Dumplin' and Tea Time Turtle	15-20	35-40+
Apricot and Hopsalot	15-20	45+
Blueberry Muffin*	15-20	40+
Huckleberry Pie*	15-20	50-55+
Lemon Meringue*	15-20	40+
Orange Blossom*	15-20	40+
Purple Pieman and Cackle	15-20	40+
Raspberry Tart*	15-20	40+
Strawberry Shortcake*	15-20	70+

Series 2

Second Issue dolls—all with pets.

Almond Tea and Marza Panda	25	50
Angel Cake and Souffle	20	40
Apple Dumplin' and Tea Time Turtle	20	40

Left: Strawberry Shortcake, Purple Pieman and Cackle, Series 2, Kenner, $40 MIP. Right: Strawberry Shortcake, Sour Grapes and Dregs the Snake, Series 2, Kenner, $50 MIP.

Strawberry Shortcake ($70 MIP) and Maple Stirrup with the Oatsmobile, Kenner.

Apricot and Hopsalot	20	40
Blueberry Muffin and Cheesecake	30	55
Butter Cookie and Jelly Bear	15	35
Cafe Ole' and Burrito	30	50
Cherry Cuddler and Gooseberry	20	30
Crepe Suzette and Eclair	35	50
Huckleberry Pie and Pupcake	25	45
Lem n' Ada and Sugarwoofer	35	50
Lemon Meringue and Frappe	30	45
Lime Chiffon and Parfait	25	40
Mint Tulip and Marsh Mallard	35	50
Orange Blossom and Marmalade	20	35
Purple Pieman and Cackle	20	40
Raspberry Tart and Rhubarb Doll	20	45
Strawberry Shortcake and Custard	25	40
Sour Grapes and Dregs the Snake	20	50

Series 3

Party Pleasers—all with pets.

Almond Tea and Marza Panda Doll	60-65	90-100+
Angel Cake and Souffle	60-65	90-100+
Apple Dumplin' and Tea Time Turtle	60-65	90-100+
Cafe O'le and Burrito	45-50	80-90+
Cherry Cuddler and Gooseberry	90-100	135-150+
Mint Tulip and Marsh Mallard	110-120	135-150+
Orange Blossom and Marmalade	60-65	90-100+
Peach Blush and Melonie Belle	95-110	135-150+
Plum Puddin' and Elderberry Owl	125-135	195-210+
Strawberry Shortcake and Custard	45-50	80-85+

Series 4

Berrykins (all with Berrykin Critters)—some of the rarest action figures ever made, and demand keeps rising.

Banana Twirl	$350	$500+
Orange Blossom	$325	$425

Left: Super Powers, Aquaman, Series 1, Kenner, 1984, $60 MIP.

Right: Super Powers, Lex Luthor, Series 1, Kenner, 1984, $15 MIP.

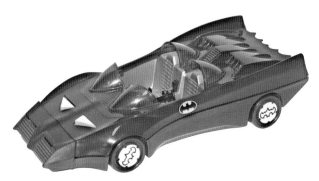

Super Powers, Batmobile, Series 1, Kenner, 1984, $160 MIP.

Super Powers, Dr. Fate, Series 2, Kenner, 1985, $50 MIP.

Left: Super Powers, Green Arrow, Series 2, Kenner, 1985, $45 MIP.

Right: Super Powers, Kalibak, Series 2, Kenner, 1985, $25 MIP.

Left: Super Powers, Mantis, Series 2, Kenner, 1985, $22 MIP.

Right: Super Powers, Martian Manhunter, Series 2, Kenner, 1985, $45 MIP.

Super Powers, Parademon, Series 2, Kenner, 1985, $22 MIP.

Left: Super Powers, Cyborg, Series 3, Kenner, 1985, $55 MIP.

Right: Super Powers, Cyclotron, Series 3, Kenner, 1985, $45 MIP.

Left: Super Powers, Mr. Miracle, Series 3, Kenner, 1985, $125 MIP.

Right: Super Powers, Orion, Series 3, Kenner, 1985, $35 MIP.

Super Powers, Plastic Man, Series 3, Kenner, 1985, $100 MIP.

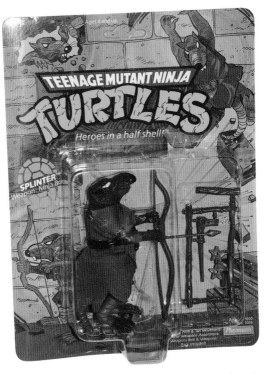

Teenage Mutant Ninja Turtles, Splinter, Series 1, Playmates, 1988, $18 MIP.

Teenage Mutant Ninja Turtles

(Playmates, 1988)

Note: There are a few variations for the 1st and 2nd Series of TMNT figures that need to be considered when gauging prices. The main four "Turtles" figures from Series 1 issued with a Fan Club Flier are the most valuable and these command $10-15 more per carded sample. Also, nine of the 1st Series figures came with "soft" plastic heads (with the exception of April O'Neil), and these usually garner $5 more per carded sample. Those nine characters with the "hard" plastic-headed versions are a bit less desirable, but still hold value.

Some series 1 and 2 characters, later versions of these carded figures, came with "pop-up display stands," and these are MUCH more desirable than their regular carded counterparts. Add $20-25 to each carded figure's price when they include a pop-up display stand. Regardless of the extras included in the TMNT packages, these toys have caught fire lately, and are quite desirable on the secondary market.

Series 1 (late 1987/early 1988)

Figures, individually carded

April O'Neil (without blue stripe on leg)	15-18	90-100
Bebop	10-12	20-25
Donatello	6-8	12-15
Foot Soldier	6-8	15-18
Leonardo	6-8	12-15
Michaelangelo	6-8	12-15
Raphael	6-8	12-15
Rocksteady	10-12	20-25
Shredder	6-8	11-13
Splinter	6-8	15-18

Vehicles and Accessories

Cheapskate	8	12-15
Knucklehead	6	10-12
Turtle Trooper	6	10-12
Turtle Blimp	20-25	35-40 (60+ MISB)
Turtle Party Wagon	12-15	25+

Teenage Mutant Ninja Turtles, April O'Neil, Series 2, Playmates, 1989, $20 MIP.

Series 2 (1989)

Figures, individually carded

April O'Neil (with blue stripe on leg)	10	20
Ace Duck (hat on)	6	12
Ace Duck (hat off)	6	22-25
Baxter Stockman	6-8	12-14
Casey Jones	6	12-15
General Traag	4	12
Genghis Frog (black belt)	4	12-15
Genghis Frog (yellow belt)	20-25	60-65
Krang	6	12
Leatherhead	6-8	12-15
Metalhead	6	12
Rat King	6	12-15
Usagi Yojimbo	6	12-15

Vehicles, Playsets, and Accessories

Army Tube	5	10-12
Crazy Artillery	5	10
Double-Barreled Plunger Gun	5	10-12
Flush-O-Matic	5	10-12
Foot Cruiser	5	12-15
Footski	5	10
Party Tube	5	10
Retrocatapault	5	10
Turtlecycle	5	10-12
Turtle Pizza Thrower	5	10
Sewer Playset	15-20	20-25 (80+ MISB)
Sewer Tubes	15-20	18-22 (45+ MISB)

Series 3 (1990)

Figures, individually carded

Fugitoid	5	12
Mondo Gecko (blue eyebrows)	5	12-15

Teenage Mutant Ninja Turtles, Scumbug, Series 3, Playmates, 1990, $12 MIP.

Chrome Dome	5	10-12
Dirtbag	6	12-15
Don "Undercover"	5	10
Groundchuck	6	12-15
Hose 'Em Down Don	5	10
Leo, the Sewer Samurai	5	10
Make My Day Leo	5	10
Mike, the Sewer Surfer	5	10
Pizzaface	5	10
Raph, the Space Cadet	5	10
Ray Fillet (blue "V")	5	10
(red "V")	6	12-15
(purple "V")	8-10	25-30
Sergeant Bananas	8-10	15-20
Space Usagi	6	10-12
Walkabout	10	25-30
Wyrm	10	22-25

Headdroppin' Turtles

Donatello, Leonardo, Michaelangelo, Raphael	5 ea.	15 ea. MOC

Large Figures

Bebop	15-20	45
Rocksteady	15-20	45

Mutant Military

Lieutenant Leo, Midshipman Mike, Pro Pilot Don, Raph the Teen Green Beret	5 ea.	10 ea. MOC

Rock 'N Roll Turtles

Rock 'N Roll Don, Leo, Mike, and Raph	5 ea.	10-12 ea. MOC

Storage Shell Turtles

Donatello, Leonardo, Michaelangelo and Raphael (all with Storage Shell)	5 ea.	10 ea MOC

Sewer Sports Turtles

Grand Slammin' Raph, Shell Kickin' Raph, Shell Slammin' Mike, Slam Dunkin' Don, Slap Shot Leo, Touchdown Tossin' Leo	5 ea.	10 ea. MOC

Talkin' Turtles

Talking Don, Talking Leo, Talking Mike, Talking Raph	5 ea.	10 ea. MOC

Wacky Action Turtle

Breadfightin' Raph	4	10
Creepy Crawlin' Splinter	4	10
Sword Slicin' Leo	4	10
Wacky Walkin' Mouser	6	12-14

Vehicles, Playsets, and Accessories

Cheapskate II	8-10	20
Don's Kookie Carnival Car	8-10	20
Don's Phone Line Rider Backpack	8-10	20
Don's Sewer Squirter	8-10	20
Leo's Turtle Trike	8-10	20
Mike's Bugchucku Set	8-10	20
Mike's Kowabunga Beachbuggy	8-10	20
Mike's Jolly Turtle Tugboat	8-10	20
Mike's Pizza Choppin' Backpack	8-10	20
Mike's Sewer Exploration Set	8-10	20
Ninja Newscycle	8-10	20
Raph's Pizza Pie Set	8-10	20
Raph's Sewer Speedboat	8-10	20
Raph's Sewer Spy Glasses	8-10	20
Raph's Turtle Dragster	8-10	20
Rocksteady's Pogocopter	8-10	20
Sewer Sub	10-15	25-30
Shell Top 4x4	20-22	45
Shreddermobile	12-15	30

Turtle Blimp II	35	50 (80+ MISB)
Turtle Communicator	8-10	20
Turtle Tank	12-15	30

Series 5 (1992)

Figures, individually carded

April (purple and yellow colors)	6-8	12-15
April, the Ravishing Reporter	6-8	12-15
April, Ninja	6-8	12-15
Antrax	9-11	15-20
Doctor El	9-11	15-20
Hothead	9-11	15-20
King Lionheart	12	20
Merdude	12	20
Monty Moose	9-11	15-20
Rahzar	6-8	12-15
Rock 'N Roll Mondo Gecko	6-8	12-15
Scale Tail	9-11	15-20
Skateboardin' Mike	6	12-15
Super Shredder	5	10
Tattoo (minus tattoo on stomach)	5	10
Tattoo (with tattoo on stomach)	12-15	25
Tokka	6-8	12-15
Zak the Neutrino	6-8	12-15

Large Figures

Grand Slam Dunkin' Don	100	300+ MISB
Movie Don, Movie Leo, Movie Mike, Movie Raph	12-15	40+ MISB

Movie Series

Movie Don, Movie Footsolider, Movie Leo, Movie Mike, Movie Raph, Movie Splinter	9-11 ea.	15-20 ea. MOC

Vehicles, Playsets, and Accessories

Bubble Bomber	7-9	18-20
Don's Pizza Powered Parachute	7-9	18-20

Lieutenant Leo's Bodacious Buggy	7-9	18-20
Muta-Bike	7-9	18-20
Muta-Raft	7-9	18-20
Muta-Ski	7-9	18-20
Mutations Muta-Carrier	10-12	20-25
Rock 'N Roll Muta-Bus	10-12	22-28
Samurai Scooter	7-9	18-20
Sewer Sandcruiser	10-12	30+
Turtlemobile	10-12	30+

Series 6 (1993)

Figures, individually carded

April O'Neil	6-8	10-12
Baxter Stockman	6-8	10-12
Foot Solider	6-8	10-12
Half Court	10-12	18-22
Hot Spot	20-25	50+
Krang	6-8	10-12
Mighty Bebop	10-12	18-22
Mona Lisa	6-8	10-12
Movie Star Splinter	6-8	10-12
Movie Star Super Shredder	6-8	10-12
Rhinoman	6-8	10-12
Robotic Bebop	8	18-20
Robotic Rocksteady	6-8	10-12
Rocksteady	6-8	10-12
Sandstorm	10-12	18-22
Scratch	120-140	350+
Super Don	10-12	18-22
Super Mike	10-12	18-22
Auto-Mutations	4-5 ea.	10-12 ea.

Cave Turtles

Don and Trippy Tyrannosaurus	10-12	18-22
Leo and Dingy Dino	10-12	18-22

Mike and Silly Stegosaurus	10-12	18-22
Raph and Turbular Pterodactyl	10-12	18-22
Mutations	4-5 ea.	10-12 ea.

Mutations, Giant Sized
Donatello, Leonardo, Michaelangelo, Raphael	12-15 ea.	40-45 ea. MISB

Ninja Action Turtles
Black Belt Boxer Mike	18-20	45-50
Cartwheelin' Karate Don	8	12-15
Jump Attack Jujitsu Raph	8	12-15
Somversaultin' Samurai Leo	8	12-15

Teenage Mutant Ninja Turtles Movie III
April O'Neil	8	12-15
Castle Guard (with Evil Warhorse)		
Kenshin		
Princess Mitsu	8	12-15
Rebel Soldier (with Warhorse)		
Samurai Don	8	12-15
Samurai Leo	8	12-15
Samurai Mike	8	12-15
Samurai Raph	8	12-15
Splinter	8	12-15
Turtle-Pault	8	12-15
Walker	8	12-15
Warlord		

12" Movie III
Samurai Leo, Samurai Raph	12-15	30-35
Toon Turtles	4-5 ea.	10-12 ea.

Universal Monsters Turtles
Donatello as Dracula	4	8
Leonardo as the Wolfman	4	8
Michaelangelo as Frankenstein's Monster	4	8
Raphael as The Mummy	8	15-20

A great assortment of LJN's Thundercats including Lion-O, Cheetara, Panthro, Tygra, Wilykit and Wilykat, 1986-87.

Mutant Masters	10-12 ea.	35-40 ea. MOC
Savage Dragon Turtles	3-4 ea.	8-10 ea. MOC
Warriors of the Forgotten Sewer	3-4 ea.	8-10 ea. MOC

Teenage Mutant Ninja Turtles
(Mattel, 2002-present)

The value on a few select figures have increased (usually on short-packed villains, etc.), but these minor price increases do not warrant a guide as of yet, as most (if not all) of these toys are still available at retail.

Teenage Mutant Ninja Turtles: The Next Mutation
(Playmates, 1997)

These figures are worth approximately what they sold for at retail in 1997— no increased value as of yet.

Teenage Mutant Ninja Turtles; Reissues
(Playmates, 1998-99)

Other than Undercover Donatello with a Cloth Coat (MLC $15-20, MOC $55-60) these are each worth approximately $2-3 ea. loose, and $5-8 ea. MOC.

Thundercats
(LJN, 1986-87)

Series 1, 6" figures (1986)

Heroes

Cheetara	20-25	200
Cheetara (with Wilykit pvc)	22-25	200
Lion-O (with free batteries)	25-30	200-230+
Lion-O (orange hair variant)	25-30	190-210+
Panthro	30-35	95-100
Tygra ("young")	40-45	95-100
Tygra ("young," with Wilykat pvc)	40-45	95-100

Thundercats, Lion-O, Series 2, LJN, 1986, $90 MIP.

Villains

Jackalman	15	25-30
Monkian	10-12	25-30
Mumm-Ra	15	55-60
Mumm-Ra (with free batteries)	15	55-60+
S-S-Slithe	12-15	25-30

Accessories

Sword of Omens	125+	300+
Creatures: Astral Moat Monster	10-15	45-50+

Vehicles

Mutant Nosediver	10-12	35-40
Mutant Skycutter	10-12	35-40
Thundertank	40-45	70-75

Series 2 (1986)

Heroes

Hachiman	10-12	30-35
Lion-O (orange hair variant w/ Snarf pvc)	25-30	110+
Lion-O (red hair variant)	25-30	90+
Tygra ("old")	22-26	75+
Tygra ("old" with Wilykat pvc)	22-26	75+
Tuska Warrior	10-12	30-35
Snowman of Hook Mountain	12-15	25-30

Villains

Grune the Destroyer	12-15	25-30
Mumm-Ra (with Ravage pvc)	15-20	65-70+
Ratar-O	10-12	25-30
Vultureman	10-12	25-30

Companions

Berbil Belle	8-12	50
Berbile Bert	8-12	50
Berbil Bill	8-12	50
Ma-Mutt	5-6	40

Snarf	8-12	45
Wilykat	12-15	60
Wilykit	12-15	60

Vehicles and Playsets

Cat's Lair	125+	300+ (MISB 500+)
Fist Pounder	15-20	50+
Hovercat	15-20	50
Mumm-Ra's Tomb Fortress	90-95	95 (150+ MISB)
Thunderclaw		

Mail-away

Mumm-Ra, "Mummy"	5-10	20+ MISB

Series 3 (1987)

Heroes

Ben Gali	75+	250+
Jaga	60+	140+
Lynx-O	35-40	125+
Pumyra	45-50	95-100

Villains

Captain Cracker	15-18	35
Captain Shiner	15-18	35
Mongor	15-20	40
Safari Joe	15-20	40

Berserkers

Cruncher	8-10	30-35
Hammerhand	10-12	30-35
Ram Bam	8-10	30-35
Topspinner	8-10	30-35

Ram-Pagers

The Driller	40-50	75-100+
The Mad Bubbler	n/a (was this even made?)	
The Stinger	55-60	125+

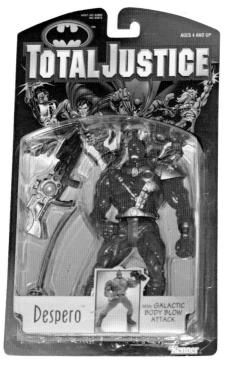

Total Justice, Despero, Series 2, Kenner, 1996, $10 MIP.

Two-Packs

Luna Lasher with Mumm-Ra	60-70+	250+
Thunderwings with Lion-O (no wings, loose Lion-O with no "Battle-Matic Action" or light-up eyes)	60-70+	250+

Creatures

Tongue-a-saurus	55-60	100+

Vehicles and Accessories

Laser Saber Backpack, Blue (good), Red (evil), Orange (good) or Black (evil)	10ea.	25 ea.

Transporters

Luna Lasher	8	15
Stilt Walker	8	15
Thunderwings	8	15

Total Justice

(Kenner, 1996-97)

Series 1 (1996), 5" Figures

Aquaman	3-5	8-10
Batman	5-8	30-35
Darkseid	3-5	8-10
Flash, The	3-5	10-12
Green Lantern	3-5	10-12
Robin	3-5	18-22

Series 2 (1996)

Batman, Fractal Armor	3-5	8-10
Despero	3-5	8-10
Hawkman	3-5	8-10
Superman	3-5	10-12

Series 3 (1997)

Black Lightning	3-5	12-15
Hunters, The	3-5	12-15

Parallax	3-5	15-18
Green Arrow	3-5	12-15
Mail-away		
Batman	10-12	20-22 (mint in baggie)
Superman	10-12	20-22 (mint in baggie)

Transformers

(Hasbro, 1984-91; 1993-present)

Transformers, Generation 1

Series 1 (1984)

No heat-sensitive "rubsigns" present, just simple silver "faction" labels and as such, finicky collectors prefer the 1984 versions of the 1984-85 Autobots and Decepticons.

Autobot Minicars		
Brawn	8-10	75-100
Bumblebee, yellow	10	85-125+
Bumblebee, red	20-25	100-125+
Bumblejumper (strange mix of Cliffjumper and Bumblebee)	50-60	350-375+
Cliffjumper, red	10	75-100+
Cliffjumper, yellow	15-20	75-100+
Gears	8-10	75-100
Huffer	8-10	65-75
Windcharger	10	65-75

Autobot Cars		
Bluestreak	65-70	300 (600+ MISB)
Hound	45-55	175 (300+ MISB)
Ironhide	45-50	125 (275+ MISB)
Jazz	55-65	175 (350+ MISB)
Mirage	60-65	150 (400+ MISB)
Prowl	60-65	225 (375+ MISB)
Ratchet (no cross)	40-45	125 (250+ MISB)

Transformers, Generation 1, Series 1, Optimus Prime, Hasbro, 1984, $275 MIP.

Ratchet (with cross)	50-55	125 (275+ MISB)
Sideswipe	55-65	150 (375+ MISB)
Sunstreaker	55-65	175 (400+ MISB)
Trailbreaker	45-55	135 (300+ MISB)
Wheeljack	45–55	135 (275+ MISB)

Autobot Commander
Optimus Prime	65-70	125 (275+ MISB)

Decepticon Cassettes
Frenzy (two-pack)	20-25	150+ (MOC, both sealed on card)
Laserbeak (two-pack)	20-25	
Ravage (two-pack)	25-35	175+ (MOC, both sealed on card)
Rumble (two-pack)	20-25	

Decepticon Communicator
Soundwave	55	125 (200+ MISB)
Buzzsaw	20-25	n/a

(comes packaged with Soundwave, above)

Decepticon Planes
Skywarp	50-60	125 (200+ MISB)
Starscream	55-65	150 (300+ MISB)
Thundercracker	50-60	125 (190+ MISB)

Decepticon Leader
Megatron	60-70	125 (275+ MISB)

Series 2 (1985)

Note: All Series 1 1984 Transformers were re-released with a heat-sensitive "rubsign" that proved Hasbro's high-quality Transformers were indeed the *real deal*. These versions of those twenty-eight Autobots (good guys) and Decepticons (bad guys)—excluding color variations, of course—are in a little bit less of demand than their regularly-labeled compatriots.

loose specimen, and $15-20 per MISB specimen), but in recent months, the demand for the pieces has prohibited a difference in price. Regardless of metal or plastic pieces, these figures are in high demand.

Note 2: The above figures that come with a "free glow-in-the-dark *Transformers: The Movie* poster" packaged in MIB or MISB samples should add $15-25 to the end price.

Sharkticon

Gnaw	60-70	80 (175+ MISB)

Note 2: The above figures that come with a "free glow-in-the-dark *Transformers: The Movie* poster"packaged in MIB or MISB samples should add $15-25 to the end price.

Stunticons

Merge to form the super-robot "Menasor."

Breakdown	15-18	55+ MOC
Dead End	15-18	55+ MOC
Drag Strip	15-18	55+ MOC
Motormaster	35-45	60+ (200+ MISB)
Wildrider	15-18	55+ MOC
Menasor Gift Set (all 5 Stunticons together)	80-95	225-250 (400+MISB)

Mail-aways

S.T.A.R.S. Autobot Command Center	65-70	100 (150+ MISB)

Series 4 (1987)

The major packing promotional for late 1987 releases were "Transformer Decoys"—smaller, either purple or red colored soft plastic PVC figures molded in the form of popular Autobots and Decepticons. These were packaged with MOC Transformers from 1987 such as smaller carded figures and carded "merge group" members (Aerialbots, Combaticons, Protectobots, Stunticons, Technobots, Terrorcons, and the smaller Throttlebots). The rarest of these decoys are Decepticons cast in red color, and any and either-colored Laserbeak or Ravage PVC Decoys (which sell for about $10-12 apiece). If any of the aforementioned characters are sealed MOC with a decoy, add about $10-15 to the MOC value, plus the value of the decoy itself based on the popularity of the PVC character, especially Laserbeak and Ravage.

Ratchet (with cross)	50-55	125 (275+ MISB)
Sideswipe	55-65	150 (375+ MISB)
Sunstreaker	55-65	175 (400+ MISB)
Trailbreaker	45-55	135 (300+ MISB)
Wheeljack	45–55	135 (275+ MISB)

Autobot Commander
Optimus Prime	65-70	125 (275+ MISB)

Decepticon Cassettes
Frenzy (two-pack)	20-25	150+ (MOC, both sealed on card)
Laserbeak (two-pack)	20-25	
Ravage (two-pack)	25-35	175+ (MOC, both sealed on card)
Rumble (two-pack)	20-25	

Decepticon Communicator
Soundwave	55	125 (200+ MISB)
Buzzsaw	20-25	n/a
	(comes packaged with Soundwave, above)	

Decepticon Planes
Skywarp	50-60	125 (200+ MISB)
Starscream	55-65	150 (300+ MISB)
Thundercracker	50-60	125 (190+ MISB)

Decepticon Leader
Megatron	60-70	125 (275+ MISB)

Series 2 (1985)

Note: All Series 1 1984 Transformers were re-released with a heat-sensitive "rubsign" that proved Hasbro's high-quality Transformers were indeed the *real deal*. These versions of those twenty-eight Autobots (good guys) and Decepticons (bad guys)—excluding color variations, of course—are in a little bit less of demand than their regularly-labeled compatriots.

Transformers, Generation 1, Series 2, Jetfire, Hasbro, 1985, $375 MISB.

Transformers, Generation 1, Series 2, Blaster, Hasbro, 1985, $225 MISB and Steeljaw, Series 3, Hasbro, 1986, $140 MOC.

Autobots

Autobot Air Guardian

Jetfire	135	220 (375+ MISB)

Autobot Cars

Bluestreak	65-70	300 (550+ MISB)
Grapple	50	125 (200+ MISB)
Hoist	45-50	125 (200+ MISB)
Hound	45-55	175 (300+ MISB)
Inferno	40-45	125 (200+ MISB)
Ironhide	45-50	125 (275+ MISB)
Jazz	55-65	175 (350+ MISB)
Mirage	60-65	150 (400+ MISB)
Prowl	60-65	225 (375+ MISB)
Ratchet (no cross)	40-45	125 (250+ MISB)
Ratchet (with cross)	50-55	125 (275+ MISB)
Red Alert	40-45	110 (225+ MISB)
Sideswipe	55-65	150 (375+ MISB)
Skids	55-70	150 (300+ MISB)
Smokescreen	45-50	125 (225+ MISB)
Sunstreaker	55-65	175 (400+ MISB)
Tracks	55-65	125 (275+ MISB)
Trailbreaker	45-55	135 (300+ MISB)
Wheeljack	45–55	135 (275+ MISB)

Autobot Communicator

Blaster	55	140 (225+ MISB)

Autobot Deluxe Vehicles

Roadbuster	75	150 (300+ MISB)
Whirl	50+	100 (250+ MISB)

Autobot Jumpstarters

Topspin	8	35-40
Twin Twist	8	35-40

Autobot Minicars

Beachcomber	8-10	30-35
Brawn	8-10	65-90
Bumblebee, yellow	10	75-115
Bumblebee, red	20-25	90-115
Cliffjumper, red	10	65-90
Cliffjumper, yellow	15-20	65-90
Cosmos	8	35
Gears	8-10	55-80
Huffer	8-10	50-65
Powerglide	8	40
Seaspray	5-6	40
Warpath	8	50
Windcharger	10	50-60

Autobot Minispies

These were sold with late-issue 1985 Autobot Minicars as an exclusive bonus for either the Autobot or Decepticon armies. These Minispies came in four different models: dune buggy, jeep, mazda, or porche. Of these four models, each model came in one of three different colors: blue, white, or yellow. That makes twelve different mini-spies available for the collector who believes in obtaining one of everything. These Minispies sell for between 5 and 8 dollars apiece, based on condition (and sometimes faction—Autobot or Decepticon). Also, an Autobot Minicar carded with a Minispy next to it is highly desirable and commands more money than regular carded Minicars.

Autobot Scientist

Perceptor	35-40	75 ($175+ MISB)

(Motorized) Autobot Defense Base

Omega Supreme	140-160	200-210 (350+ MISB)

Dinobots

Grimlock	35	125 (300+ MISB)
Slag	40	100 (225+ MISB)

Sludge	40	125 (250+ MISB)
Snarl	40	125 (270+ MISB)
Swoop	55-65	250 (450+ MISB)

Mail-away Omnibots
Camshaft	20-25	25-35 MISP
Downshift	20-25	25-35 MISP
Overdrive	20-25	25-35 MISP

Mail-away Powerdashers
Car	20-22	45-50 MISP
Drill	15-20	45-50 MISP
Jet	20-25	45-50 MISP

Watch
| Time Traveller | 35-40 | 65-70 MISP |

Decepticons

Constructicons
Merge to form the super-robot "Devastator."

Bonecrusher	15-20	65-70
Hook	15-20	65-70
Long Haul	15-20	65-70
Mixmaster	15-20	65-70
Scavenger	15-20	65-70
Scrapper	15-20	65-70
Devastator Gift Set		
(all 6 Constructicons together)	95-115	160-180 (375+MISB)

Decepticon Cassettes
Frenzy	(two-pack)	20-25
		175+ (MOC, both sealed on card)
Laserbeak (two-pack)	20-25	
Ravage (two-pack)	25-35	175+ (MOC, both sealed on card)
Rumble (two-pack)	20-25	

Decepticon Communicator

Soundwave	55	125 (250+ MISB)
Buzzsaw	20-25	n/a (comes packaged with Soundwave, above)

Decepticon Military Operations Commander

Shockwave	110-125	160-175 (315+ MISB)

Decepticon Planes

Dirge	30-35	65-70 (150+ MISB)
Ramjet	50-60	70-75 (175+ MISB)
Skywarp	50-60	125 (210+ MISB)
Starscream	55-65	150 (325+ MISB)
Thrust	55-65	125 (225+ MISB)
Thundercracker	50-60	125 (210+ MISB)

Decepticon Leader

Megatron	60-70	125 (325+ MISB)

Deluxe Insecticons

Barrage	30-40	60 (110+ MISB)
Chop Shop	30-40	60 (110+ MISB)
Ransack	30-40	60 (110+ MISB)
Venom	30-40	60 (110+ MISB)

Insecticons

Bombshell	20	40 (95-100 MISB)
Kickback	20	40 (95-100 MISB)
Shrapnel	20	40 (95-100 MISB)

Triple Changers

Astrotrain	30-35	75-80 (200+ MISB)
Blitzwing	35-40	75-80 (200+ MISB)

Mail-away

Decepticon Camera		
Reflector (Spectro, Spyglass, Viewfinder)	150-180	250 (300+ MISB)

Spectro, individual figure	38-40	
Spyglass, individual figure	38-40	
Viewfinder, individual figure	50-55	

Series 3 (1986)

Autobots

Aerialbots
Merge to form the super-robot "Superion."

Air Raid	15-20	55+ MOC
Fireflight	15-20	55+ MOC
Silverbolt	35-40	120 (220 MISB)
Slingshot	10-15	55+ MOC
Skydive	10-15	55+ MOC
Superion Gift Set (all 5 Aerialbots together)	95-115	175-200 (375+ MISB)

Autobot Battle Station

Metroplex (rubber or plastic tires)	110-125	165-180 (400+ MISB)

The above figure with a "free glow-in-the-dark *Transformers: The Movie* poster" packaged in a MIB or MISB sample should add $15-25 to the price.

Autobot Cars

Blurr	25-35	100 (200+ MISB)
Hot Rod (metal or plastic toes)	50-60	200 (350+ MISB)
Kup	22-28	100 (200+ MISB)

The above figures that came with a "free glow-in-the-dark *Transformers: The Movie* poster" in packaged MIB or MISB samples should add $15-25 to the end prices.

Autobot Cassettes

Rewind (two-pack)	22-25	150+ (MOC, both sealed on card)
Steeljaw (two-pack)	20-22	
Eject (two-pack)	22-25	150+ (MOC, both sealed on card)
Ramhorn (two-pack)	22-25	

Note: the figures above have "gold" chromed weapons.

Eject (two-pack)	20-22	140+ (MOC, both sealed on card)
Ramhorn (two-pack)	18-20	
Rewind (two-pack)	20-22	140+ (MOC, both sealed on card)
Steeljaw (two-pack)	18-20	

Note: the figures above have "silver" chromed weapons.

Autobot City Commander

Ultra Magnus (rubber or plastic tires)	50-55	70-80 (160+ MISB)

The above figure with a "free glow-in-the-dark *Transformers: The Movie* poster" packaged in a MIB or MISB sample should add $15-25 to the end price.

Autobot Heroes

Rodimus Prime (metal or plastic toes)	55-60	75-80 (175+ MISB)
Wreck Gar	45-50	70-75 (160+ MISB)

The above figures with a "free glow-in-the-dark *Transformers: The Movie* poster" packaged in MIB or MISB samples should add $15-25 to the end prices.

Autobot Minicars

Note: All Minicars released in 1985 were re-released MOC with a free promotional Iron-On Patch included in the package. This does not raise the price of carded specimens (see *Autobot Minicars*, 1985). These Iron-Ons sell for $2-5 apiece depending upon the character.

Hubcap	8	40
Outback	8-10	55
Pipes	8	45
Swerve	8	45
Tailgate	8	50

Autobot (Motorized) Space Shuttle

Sky Lynx		
(electronics don't work)	35-45	70-95
(working electronics)	70-80	85-120 (325+ MISB)

The above figures with a "free glow-in-the-dark *Transformers: The Movie* poster" packaged in MIB or MISB samples should add $15-25 to the end prices.

Autobot Triple Changers

Broadside	25-30	55 (130+ MISB)
Sandstorm	30-35	55 (130+ MISB)
Springer	50-55	75-80 (185+ MSIB)

Protectobots
Merge to form the super-robot "Defensor."

Blades	12-15	50+ MOC
First Aid	15-18	50+ MOC
Groove	12-15	50+ MOC
Hot Spot	30-35	65 (150+ MISB)
Streetwise	15-18	50+ MOC
Defensor Gift Set (all 5 Protectobots together)	95-120	235 (450+ MISB)

Decepticons

Battle Chargers

Runabout	8-10	40-45
Runamuck	8-10	40-45

Combaticons
Merge to form the super-robot "Bruticus."

Blast Off	15-22	60+ MOC
Brawl	12-15	50+ MOC
Onslaught	30-35	65 (150+ MISB)
Swindle	12-15	55+ MOC
Vortex	18-25	65+ MOC
Bruticus Gift Set (all 5 Combaticons together; foreign made only)	95-115	225+ (450+ MISB)

Decepticon Cassettes

Frenzy (two-pack)	20-25	200+ (MOC, both sealed on card)
Ratbat (two-pack)	35-40	

Note: the figures above have "gold" chromed weapons.

| Frenzy (two-pack) | 20-25 | 175+ (MOC, both sealed on card) |
| Ratbat (two-pack) | 30-32 | |

Note: the figures above have "silver" chromed weapons.

Decepticon City

Trypticon		
(electronics don't work)	85	145-165 (n/a)
(working electronics)	110-125	175-190 (500+ MISB)

Decepticon City Commander

| Galvatron | 55-65 | 75 (250+ MISB) |

The above figures with a "free glow-in-the-dark *Transformers: The Movie* poster" packaged in MIB or MISB samples should add $15-25 to the end prices.

Decepticon Jets

| Cyclonus | 55-60 | 65-70 (200+ MISB) |
| Scourge | 45-50 | 60-65 (200+ MISB) |

The above figures with a "free glow-in-the-dark *Transformers: The Movie* poster" packaged in MIB or MISB samples should add $15-25 to the end prices.

Decepticon Triple Changers

| Octane | 50-55 | 75-80 (190+ MISB) |

Predacons

Merge to form the super-robot "Predaking."

Divebomb	50	80 (175+ MISB)
Headstrong	50-55	80-85 (175+ MISB)
Rampage	40-45	65-70(175+ MISB)
Razorclaw	45-50	75 (175+ MISB)
Tantrum	40-45	65 (145+ MISB)
Predaking Gift Set		
(all 5 Predacons together)	190-210	275 (450+ MISB)

Note 1: The above figures came with die-cast metal parts or full plastic parts. Usually, the metal versions sell for more money (add $5 more per

loose specimen, and $15-20 per MISB specimen), but in recent months, the demand for the pieces has prohibited a difference in price. Regardless of metal or plastic pieces, these figures are in high demand.

Note 2: The above figures that come with a "free glow-in-the-dark *Transformers: The Movie* poster" packaged in MIB or MISB samples should add $15-25 to the end price.

Sharkticon

Gnaw	60-70	80 (175+ MISB)

Note 2: The above figures that come with a "free glow-in-the-dark *Transformers: The Movie* poster" packaged in MIB or MISB samples should add $15-25 to the end price.

Stunticons

Merge to form the super-robot "Menasor."

Breakdown	15-18	55+ MOC
Dead End	15-18	55+ MOC
Drag Strip	15-18	55+ MOC
Motormaster	35-45	60+ (200+ MISB)
Wildrider	15-18	55+ MOC
Menasor Gift Set (all 5 Stunticons together)	80-95	225-250 (400+MISB)

Mail-aways

S.T.A.R.S. Autobot Command Center	65-70	100 (150+ MISB)

Series 4 (1987)

The major packing promotional for late 1987 releases were "Transformer Decoys"—smaller, either purple or red colored soft plastic PVC figures molded in the form of popular Autobots and Decepticons. These were packaged with MOC Transformers from 1987 such as smaller carded figures and carded "merge group" members (Aerialbots, Combaticons, Protectobots, Stunticons, Technobots, Terrorcons, and the smaller Throttlebots). The rarest of these decoys are Decepticons cast in red color, and any and either-colored Laserbeak or Ravage PVC Decoys (which sell for about $10-12 apiece). If any of the aforementioned characters are sealed MOC with a decoy, add about $10-15 to the MOC value, plus the value of the decoy itself based on the popularity of the PVC character, especially Laserbeak and Ravage.

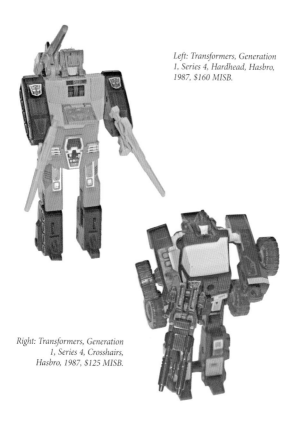

Left: Transformers, Generation 1, Series 4, Hardhead, Hasbro, 1987, $160 MISB.

Right: Transformers, Generation 1, Series 4, Crosshairs, Hasbro, 1987, $125 MISB.

Autobots

Autobot Clones

Cloudraker	13-16	50
		(110+ MISB; both clones packaged together)
Fastlane	13-16	

Autobot Double Spy

Punch/Counterpunch	32-38	60 (120+ MISB)

Autobot Headmasters

Brainstorm	50	80 (175+ MISB)
Chromedome	45	75 (160+ MISB)
Hardhead	50	75 (160+ MISB)
Highbrow	50-55	75 (180+ MISB)

Autobot Targetmasters

Blurr	50-55	175 (300+ MISB)
Crosshairs	45-50	75 (125+ MISB)
Hot Rod	65-75	300 (550+ MISB)
Kup	45-50	175 (300+ MISB)
Pointblank	45-50	75 (125+ MISB)
Sureshot	45-50	75 (125+ MISB)

Monsterbots

Doublecross	35-40	55 (100+ MISB)
Grotescue	40-45	55 (100+ MISB)
Repugnus	40-45+	55 (120+ MISB)

Technobots

Merge to form the super-robot "Computron."

Afterburner	18-24	50+ MOC
Lightspeed	18-24	50+ MOC
Nosecone	12-15	45+ MOC
Scattershot	42-48	60 (130+ MISB)
Strafe	18-24	55+ MOC